Parenting a prodigal is a tough and mostly thankless task. And too often it is lonely. I can attest to that fact that prayer is what sustains me—often at three in the morning when all I can utter is "Help!" This book of prayers for prodigals isn't just a handy tool; it's a reminder we are not alone. Written with transparent honesty and love—and straight from the trenches—it's a sincere and much-needed comfort to a parent's aching heart.

—Melody Carlson, award-winning author of more than 200 books
including *Lost Boys and the Moms Who Love Them*

*

Every time you look at your child, you know you have a problem. And everyone seems to have an "if I were you…" answer.

"Get tough," one says. "Be strict enough to force him to change."

"She is no longer a child," another admonishes. "Don't baby her."

You know you have a problem. You know you must do something. But what?

In this powerful little book, Linda Clare—who understands your conflict firsthand—shares her reason for hope.

—Kay Marshall Strom, award-winning author and
twenty-first century abolitionist

*

Prayers for Parents of Prodigals offers readers honesty, encouragement, and much-needed word

W0010467

experience. This devotional is perfect for anyone navigating the often-tumultuous journey of prodigals. This will bring solace and much-needed hope.

—Mary DeMuth, author of *Healing Every Day*

*

Prayers for Parents of Prodigals walks through the pain, agony, and heartbreak of loving a child who shatters boundaries designed to protect. Linda Clare's transparency and authentic cries to the Lord will inspire and comfort the squeezing of your heart. Her raw authenticity, like balm on an open wound, offers a soft place to land while waiting to celebrate the return of the prodigal child. As you cautiously wait to exhale, her wisdom restores like a rescue breath.

Stop. Rest your soul. Allow each prayer to rebuild your hope.

—PJ Vincent, www.pamalajvincent.com,
The Modern Woman's Life magazine

PRAYERS
for
PARENTS
of
PRODIGALS

LINDA S. CLARE

HARVEST HOUSE PUBLISHERS
EUGENE, OREGON

Prayers for Parents of Prodigals
Copyright © 2019 by Linda Clare
Published by Harvest House Publishers
Eugene, Oregon 97408
www.harvesthousepublishers.com

ISBN 978-0-7369-7901-6 (pbk.)
ISBN 978-0-7369-7902-3 (eBook)

Printed in the United States of America

19 20 21 22 23 24 25 26 27 / VP-RD / 10 9 8 7 6 5 4 3 2 1

For my three sons
and for every prodigal
trying to find the way back home.

Contents

Foreword

Prodigal is one of those words with curious definitions. One of them is "recklessly wasteful" while a second is "profuse in giving or exceedingly abundant"! Linda Clare's remarkable prayers for parents of prodigals have captured this dichotomy. Parents—and grandparents, aunts, and uncles—deeply love these children, though they are "recklessly wasteful" of the abundance God has given. Yet in the rhythm of recovery and relapse, prodigals often return to us full of remorse, abundant in their gratitude that we have stood with them, genuine in their hope that this time it will be different. We share that hope—knowing that it may not last, praying that it will.

I've heard the stories as a therapist and lived the struggle with prodigal children: visited them in jail, cared for grandchildren while they healed, wondered where we went wrong and what we could have done differently. It can be a lonely time. Linda's prayers remind us that we need to tend ourselves extravagantly and seek faith communities to be renewed for that next moment of new beginning with our prodigals. Though my husband and I have celebrated for 15 years with prodigal lives "profuse in giving," Linda's prayers are a reminder that life takes twists and turns, and God is always with us, loving us and our prodigals more deeply than we ever could.

I hope you write in the margins of these prayers and let God's grace come to you in the most personal of ways. May they bless you and your prodigal.

Jane Kirkpatrick, mental health professional, bestselling author of *One More River to Cross.*

Introduction

I never thought I'd be a parent to one prodigal child—much less three of them. I grew up middle-class with one sister, and although I was a teensy bit rebellious in my teens, Sis and I were largely compliant. We did our chores, went to school, and excelled in extracurricular activities. I was the brainiac and my sister was the athlete. Perfect.

Maybe that's why God blessed me with one daughter and three stubborn and strong-willed boys. To say I had no clue about raising sons is an understatement. When the boys each veered off into the addiction that runs rampant through both my family and my husband's family, we were flummoxed. Our middle son's meth addiction began, unbeknownst to us, around sixth or seventh grade. The other two boys followed with drug experimentation, finally settling on alcohol as their drug of choice.

Over many years, we've tried everything: keeping our family intact, despite soaring divorce rates; taking our children to church and Scout activities; giving the boys tough love and bringing them to legal venues, treatment centers, and 12-step meetings. We've cried a lot.

So far, nothing has worked. I have prayed harder, begged God more often, promised and bribed, set boundaries, and even called the police when necessary. But they are still stuck.

Years later, I've finally learned that they never thought they'd grow up to be addicts either. Addiction is not just a poor choice, but also a cruel brain disease—one that sucks the life out of both addicts and those who love them. Recovery is really hard, but it's not impossible. We've had periods of sobriety followed by many relapses. The hardest part is staying hopeful in the midst of the storm called "addiction."

Of course, parents of prodigals deal with much more than addiction. Whether it's gender-identity-based or one of a host of other hot-button morality issues, we parents all end up in the same place with the same two needs: We all need to have hope that our kids will come back to us. And to keep that hope alive, we all need something to lean on.

The only thing keeping *me* going is Jesus. Time after time, his love, comfort, and mercies have saved me from giving up hope. I've learned not to count on being delivered *out* of this nightmare—only carried through it. God loves my prodigals more than I do, and Jesus carries me when I can't go on. When circumstances go from bad to worse, and crisis scrambles my brain, a short "SOS" prayer is the best I can do.

I pray your prodigal has already looked over his or her shoulder and is heading back home today. If not, don't give up. You are not alone. God's love for each of us cannot be broken. He is always with us, and we can be there for each other.

If your life is like mine—one step forward and three steps back—I hope these short prayers will help you reconnect to God's divine love. If you recognize yourself in these scenarios, cry with me. If you've done dumb things, too, laugh. But don't *ever* give up.

Take care of yourself, parent. Keep hoping, keep praying, keep loving. Many other parents walk this difficult path with you. Jesus is always there, slogging along beside us, helping us keep hope alive. May God bless you—and your prodigals too.

I

Heartbreak

The first time your parental heart breaks because of a prodigal's behavior, you know you'll never be the same. But you'll probably never again feel as gobsmacked as the first time your child wanders. Gradually your heart papers over the hurt and hope rekindles. Until your prodigal crushes you again. And again.

One minute you're walking in sunlight, the next falling into a deep well. How do you keep hoping when all seems lost? Love for your child holds your heart together like duct tape. But when your heart breaks for the millionth time, you need something bigger. Someone bigger. To reclaim lost hope, we can grab God's hand, find comfort in Jesus, and obey the Spirit's promptings—even when our prodigal still seems far away.

Broken Heart, Broken Parent

He heals the brokenhearted
and binds up their wounds.

PSALM 147:3

Dear Lord, I can't imagine *not* loving my child—even though she's all grown up. My love runs deep, swift, and wide, but watching my child following the wrong path cuts straight through my heart, breaking it again and again. Oh, how it hurts to watch my prodigal suffer and struggle and yet still not turn back to what is right. I feel trapped inside a bad dream, with no one to turn to for comfort. It's as if my child is broken, and I feel broken too.

Lord, just as you are our heavenly Father, you know that I still love my child—whether my prodigal's waywardness is about relationships or drugs or gambling or something even worse. You know how deep the hurt goes, Lord, and how my heart's been shattered into a million pieces. Gather me under your wings. When I cry, wrap your loving arms around me. Fill me with gratitude at the knowledge that you specialize in mending broken lives. Let me always remember that you alone have the perfect answers to heal broken prodigals—and broken parents too.

I Feel So Alone

This is why I weep
and my eyes overflow with tears.
No one is near to comfort me,
no one to restore my spirit.

LAMENTATIONS 1:16

Lord, I feel so alone. My prodigal's behavior breaks my heart again and again. Just when I think the situation can't get worse—it does. The hurt is crippling me, but when others ask me how I'm doing, I often lie and say I'm fine. Truth is, I really don't want even friends or family to know how messy my life has become. What if people gossip or look down on us? What if they shun us? Times like these, I feel abandoned, alone.

When it feels like I'm flying solo, help me remember your promises, Lord God. The Israelites of old felt alone, too, wandering through the desert, but you sustained them with manna. You guided them by day and by night, all the way to the Promised Land. People don't always understand tough situations like weeping for a prodigal, but you do. Your compassion is a healing balm. When I feel alone, let me reach for your hand and hold on tight. Let me stand tall on your rock of compassion as you lovingly wipe away all my tears.

Holy Laughter

Blessed are you who weep now,
for you will laugh.

Luke 6:21

There's nothing funny about my prodigal's behavior, Lord. I've trained up my kid in the way she should go, but still she heads in the opposite direction. I've worried, begged, shouted, and cajoled my child into turning her life around, but she laughs and says my nose turns red when I'm angry. I've talked myself blue in the face, but my prodigal still has a bad attitude.

And if I think about it, Lord, maybe my attitude could use an adjustment too. In my concern, give me wisdom to judge with love. Prevent me from condemning my prodigal as I rail against her dangerous behaviors. Help me remember that mercy trumps judgment. Although my prodigal makes me cry now, help me keep hoping that I *will* laugh. Most of all, Lord, remind me not to take myself too seriously—the situation may not be funny, but my prodigal and I can both laugh at my bright red nose.

Birth Pangs of Joy

A woman giving birth has pain because her time has come; but when her baby is born she forgets the anguish because of her joy that a child is born into the world. So with you: Now is your time of grief, but I will see you again and you will rejoice, and no one will take away your joy.

JOHN 16:21-22

Babies are your miracle, God. The day I met my child, I prayed for health and ten fingers and toes. Back then, I said all that mattered was that my baby be born healthy, and you granted my request. I fell in love with that child at first sight and told him how much God loved him too. As I prayed for my child to love you, I never once imagined him becoming a prodigal.

Now, years later, my precious prodigal's health is in real danger. Whether he has an addiction, mental health issues, or a host of other problems, my child's spiritual health is failing. And as I run after him, my own health—mental, physical, and emotional—suffers too. We *both* need your healing touch, Lord. Help us seek out help, whether it comes from the faith, medical, or psychological community. Snatch us away from the precipice of unhealthy living. Restore our health, Lord, and let us forget our grief as we press forward to joy.

2

Crisis

In a crisis, it's easy to develop tunnel vision. Fire escapes or disaster plans provide automatic responses when it's too chaotic to think. Whether you're a crier or more stoic as a parent of a prodigal, you can better keep a cool head during a crisis with a plan too.

Discuss a family plan of action for the next time a crisis arises—but do it when life is relatively calm. It's up to you whether to include your prodigal, but all other family members need a job they agree to do if "prodigal chaos" breaks out. Set a behavior threshold that automatically triggers a call to the police or medical services, such as threats of self-harm or physical violence to others. By deciding in advance how you will respond to a crisis, you may stay clearheaded enough to pray.

Through the Valley

Weeping may stay for the night,
but rejoicing comes in the morning.

PSALM 30:5

Nights are the hardest. After dark, worry and fear loom so much larger. So many times I've lain awake, worrying about my prodigal child. It doesn't matter if my baby is seven or seventy—when my child is wandering far from home, I fear the nightmare will never end. Will my prodigal ever again be the amazing person I once knew? I've cried so many tears, Lord. Right now, I admit that this situation looks as black as a starless night. I feel discouraged and abandoned.

Lord, help me remember that you will never leave me. When I cry out for help, you lean down and comfort me. When I'm scared to death, you whisper that you're right there beside me. Your light cuts through the thickest night, the blackest outlook, the worst heartache. How can I think I'm alone when you are there? I need you, God, more than ever. My heart aches for my prodigal, but it also longs for you, Lord. Fill me with a peace I can't really describe. Then, somehow, I can face another day. At dawn, let me be glad that, with you by my side, morning does come.

I Hate Reruns

In this world you will have trouble.
But take heart! I have overcome the world.

JOHN 16:33

Life with a prodigal seems to run in late-night cycles. Something terrible happens—he acts out, so I'm forced to call the police; I discover she's been stealing things again; he calls me foul names—and all I can do is pray and beg you to get me through the night. Then life calms down. Promises are made. He'll never do it again; she'll get clean and stay sober; he is so very sorry. My prodigal shapes up—for a while. But it's like watching the same awful television rerun again and again. We do a dance where we edge toward better times, only to slump back again. If my prodigal says or does anything that brings me hope, I start worrying when the other shoe will drop and the cycle will go bad again.

My prodigal relapses, gets clean, and relapses again—and frankly, Lord, so do I. Help us each examine the reasons why we are both stuck in our patterns. Why won't she get help? Why can't I stand by the consequences I've laid out for him? Lord, why *do* we break promises? I think for most of us, it's fear. Fear of change, fear of the work it takes to turn from our old ways. Give both of us strength to overcome our fear of change. When crisis hits again, help us change the channel from sick rerun to new life in you.

No Doormats

Who shall separate us from the love of Christ?
Shall trouble or hardship or persecution or
famine or nakedness or danger or sword?

ROMANS 8:35

So many nights I've sat shaking, doubting I would live through another prodigal crisis. The pain of my prodigal's bad behavior and poor choices cuts so deep, I've been sure I wouldn't survive. My heart has tried to tear itself in two—one side hating the situation, the other still full of a mother's love. In error I've thought I had to choose between them, and my motherly love has won. But I don't want to be a doormat.

As I grow closer to you, Lord, I see that my unconditional love for my child doesn't mean I must unconditionally accept bad behaviors in order to keep loving him. Even though you hate sin, your love for me and my prodigal is unbreakable. I pray that I can remember, even in those horrible crisis moments, that I can still love my prodigal no matter what he does or says. But I don't have to accept his hurtful behaviors and choices. Lord, give me courage and wisdom to love my prodigal while standing strong for what's right. Help me remember that as you love me no matter what, I can love my prodigal without allowing him to wipe his feet on my heart.

Unbearable

Out of the depths I cry to you, LORD.

PSALM 130:1

Just when I think my prodigal's actions and choices can't get worse, they do. A lot worse. Times like this, I feel as if I'm stranded in a deep chasm, pinned between my parental love and the pain of the latest crisis. In the abyss, I've already exhausted every way I know to fix the situation: rescuing, minimizing, covering up, even outright lying. The only way I could go lower is if, heaven forbid, my prodigal died. With my arms wrapped tight around my middle, I moan and weep and wail. The pain is too much, Lord. I can't take it anymore.

Lord, help me see my way out of this dark canyon. When I'm hopeless, hear my cries from the deepest place in me. When I can't take any more, comfort me like a soothing, warm tea. Throw me a rope so I can start to climb out—a rope made of your love. As I climb, help me go easy on myself as my eyes again adjust to the light. Lord, help me cling to you. You're the only one who can give me the courage to bear the unbearable.

3

Worry

Eliminating worry is tough for anybody—but especially for parents of prodigals. Instead of following a cycle of worry, guilt, and more worry, lessen the burden with these tips:

- *Keep a worry journal.* List your worries as they occur to you throughout the day, praying briefly over each concern as it arises.

- *Set aside worry time.* Plan to worry at a set time. Use your worry journal or be spontaneous but worry only during this time.

- *Plan for the "awful."* Ask yourself, "What's the worst thing that could happen if my worry comes true?" If this awful outcome does happen, what will you do? Giving yourself a plan can help you realize that although you'd prefer not to experience the awful, you'll make it through.

- *Revisit the "Serenity Prayer" by Reinhold Niebuhr.* If you can't change something, why worry? It's in God's hands.

- *Practice "casting your cares" upon the Lord.* (See Psalm 55:22 and 1 Peter 5:7.) Even if you take back your worry, keep handing it over to Jesus as many times as necessary.

Worry Me Not

Will all your worries add a single moment to your life?

MATTHEW 6:27 TLB

Lord, we parents of prodigals spend a lot of time practicing our worry skills, and often for good reason. When our children first begin to wander, we hope it's a phase, but we worry it's not. As time goes on, we worry our adult prodigals will miss work and lose jobs, relationships, possessions, freedom, or even life itself. The fact is, even though I love my adult children, I have little control over their behaviors. Maybe that's why, over and over, Scripture reminds me to *fear not.*

Lord, without your help I can't stop worrying about my prodigal's situation. When I worry about things I can't control—like my prodigal—I'm really saying I can't trust you to work things out. Then I worry even more. I need reassurance, Lord. I'll pray for my child's healing. But help me remember that *you* desire his healing too—and that I need not worry about your timing or methods. Whenever worry begins to creep back in, let me whisper, "Fear not."

Dead-End Worry Pit

God rescued us from dead-end alleys and dark dungeons.
He's set us up in the kingdom of the Son he loves so
much, the Son who got us out of the pit we were in, got
rid of the sins we were doomed to keep repeating.

COLOSSIANS 1:13-14 MSG

The more I examine my worries, the more they seem like a waste of time. I recycle fears that my prodigal child will do this or that or won't do what I want him to do. When any of these fears comes to pass, it feels as if I got a perfect score on the worry test. If I'm afraid she'll become homeless, end up in jail, or lose her marriage, and it happens, what have I done besides waste a chance to pray for God's outcome? If I worry he'll steal from me or spend his pay on drugs or alcohol, and instead he stays sober and pays his bills, what good was all my worry?

Lord, I pray that you'll help me trade a habit of worry for a habit of prayer. In Scripture we're never admonished to worry more. No, we're encouraged to pray without ceasing. I can see that worry is a dark dungeon, a bottomless pit. Help me look to Jesus any time I'm tempted to climb back into the Worry Pit. Help me learn to pray for my prodigal and kick worry to the curb.

Down with Worry

*I am leaving you with a gift—peace of mind and
heart! And the peace I give isn't fragile like the peace
the world gives. So don't be troubled or afraid.*

JOHN 14:27 TLB

When worry about my prodigal consumes me, I start
a downhill slide into depression on broken skis shaped
like the word *why*. Why won't my child stop hurting
himself and me with his behavior? Why won't she accept
responsibility for the pain she's caused? Why doesn't he
want drug, alcohol, or mental-health treatment? Why,
Lord, why?

Lord, help me see that the more I worry, the more dangerous and conflicted my own state of mind becomes.
Help me let go of the whys that keep sending me plung-
ing down the mountain of depression. Give me courage to seek help if my depression lingers or grows worse,
or if I start thinking about harming myself. Help me
instead become consumed with your goodness, mercy,
and loving compassion, drinking in your love like a
warm cup of cocoa on a cold winter's day. Let me trade
in my *why* skis for the gift you've promised—"peace of
mind and heart."

Hold My Hand

Do not be afraid, for I am with you.

GENESIS 26:24

Sometimes, Lord, worry gets the best of me. Okay, a lot of times. I worry when people ask me why I don't make my prodigal go to treatment. I worry people are gossiping about my family or looking down on us. My prodigal's life is slipping away—and I worry she won't be able to correct her course in time. I worry I'm not a good enough parent, and I worry I don't worry often enough or in the right way.

Help me, Lord. All these worries are for things I can't or shouldn't control. I can't "make" my prodigal get clean or do what others think he should do. If people gossip about us or shun me, help me remember that your love will always be there for me. If I take worry to ridiculous levels, I pray for your gentle nudge, the one that says, "I am with you." Help both my child and me feel your presence as we face worry head-on and banish it from our hearts and minds. Give me strength to remember that learning not to worry is easier if I keep my thoughts on heavenly truths.

4

Guilt

Like never-ending baskets of dirty laundry, guilt tends to pile up around parents of prodigals. If only we'd done more, said less, taught this, forbidden that. But how can we separate true guilt from false guilt?

True guilt implies intentional behavior—you knew better, but you acted or spoke wrongly or thought negatively about your prodigal. God is the only stain remover who can take away true guilt. False guilt spins truth like an off-balance washing machine, trying to trick you into accepting responsibility for something that isn't yours. False guilt dances across the floor, loudly accusing you until you pull its plug.

If you feel guilty over your ability to control your child past a certain age, then bingo—you're harboring false guilt. Let it go. Have you also actively loved your child, taught her as well as you could, given her opportunities according to your resources? Have you tried your best to teach your child to love God and her neighbor? If you answer, "Yes," then you're truly guilty—guilty of loving your child.

Be Not Sorry

My guilt has overwhelmed me like a burden too heavy to bear.

PSALM 38:4

"I'm sorry." My loved ones claim I say it way too often, Lord. No matter what goes wrong, I apologize. If my prodigal doesn't like the meal I prepared, I'm sorry that I'm a bad cook. If I'm a minute late to pick her up, I'm sorry. I've even said sorry to the cops who had to come to the house during a crisis. All these sorries add up to feelings of guilt. I'm guilty of not pleasing my prodigal—when many times he wouldn't be happy no matter what I did. This is the definition of false guilt. The idea that I'm responsible for another person's mood is silly, especially when it involves a prodigal who manipulates, lies, or thrives on drama. But as silly as it sounds, I claim false guilt daily, chanting, "Sorry, sorry, sorry." Even worse, the more I feel guilty for failing my prodigal, the more my hope drains away.

God, I'm suffocating under a burden of guilt that isn't even mine. False guilt not only squeezes the hope out of me, but it also nurtures a sick attitude that's really about pride. Help me recognize that false guilt presumes I'm responsible for everything and everybody. I need your grace to admit that, in a strange way, this guilt makes me feel needed and important. Help me practice accepting guilt only for my own errors. Let me confess my mistakes before you, Lord, and then let me learn and go forward. Let me draw close to Jesus, where hope can grow. Then my burden will be light.

Finger Pointers

Take away the disgrace I dread,
for your laws are good.

Psalm 119:39

Anytime an acquaintance finds out I'm a parent of a prodigal, I cringe. The phony mask I've presented to the world—the one that claims we're a perfect, talented, successful family—suddenly falls away. I'm left making excuses or defending my child and our circumstances, especially if the other person's kid seems to have it all. Then guilt lands on my head like a dive-bombing crow, and I can't get away fast enough. Even if I tell myself that they just don't understand, or that I tried my best, I feel guilty. I end up ignoring or justifying places where I *am* guilty while accepting fault for situations I can't control. I'm wearing a sign that reads, "I'm the world's biggest failure—and lawbreaker too."

But, Lord, I *did* try my best. I trained up my child in the way he should go—it's just that as he got older, he didn't go that way. Remind me that if I see my faith only through the eyes of the law, I'll feel stuck with a mountain of guilt. Help me see life through Jesus' eyes—eyes that remind us that we are under grace, not the law. Lord, help me reject false guilt that was never mine to begin with.

Real Love

*Guard my life and rescue me; do not let me
be put to shame, for I take refuge in you.*

PSALM 25:20

Guilt over my prodigal's behavior can lead to self-pity—
and misery. If I rescue my prodigal or tell the world
what a victim I am, I'm not helping anybody. If I insist
on staying in "safe" mode—that is, not rocking the
boat for fear of what my prodigal might do, smooth-
ing over a tough situation instead of making a plan and
acting on it—then I really *am* guilty. Guilty of per-
petuating a terrible cycle of helping, feeling used, and
feeling bad until the next time. Others who point out
my responsibility in the cycle might get my anger in
return—and later on, I feel guilty for that too. I admit
that oftentimes my attempts to rescue my prodigal
really help *me* the most, at least in the moment. Breaking the cycle requires my participation—I'll need to
change as much as my prodigal.

Lord, I don't want to live in Victimville. When I seek
to rescue or help my prodigal, give me wisdom to be
honest about my motives. You know I love my child as
only a parent can. Help me put an end to my tendency
to think love always means getting my prodigal out of
a jam or ignoring his waywardness. Guard my heart
against the desire to rescue my prodigal only so I won't

have to watch her suffer. Help me instead take refuge in your love and, in doing so, show my prodigal real love. Because that's where real love hangs out. With your help, Lord, that's where I want to be.

God's Free Pass

Let us go right in to God himself, with true hearts
fully trusting him to receive us because we have been
sprinkled with Christ's blood to make us clean and
because our bodies have been washed with pure water.

HEBREWS 10:22 TLB

If I'm sincerely willing to face the guilt from my own mistakes and try to turn away from unhealthy behaviors, Lord God, you make it easy. My prodigal's behavior still cuts deep—it's like walking on razor blades. But by owning only *my* part in it, I'm able to run straight into Jesus' arms for comfort, guilt free, by virtue of his sacrifice once for all. Clinging to Jesus, my scrambled thinking begins to clarify. I'm not guilty of being a lousy parent although I confess I certainly have sinned as a parent. I *am* guilty of loving my child. Yet I'm beginning to understand how repeating the same rescues and fixes—covering up mistakes, replacing lost possessions, paying fines—and then feeling guilty about it helps no one at all. One piece of true guilt I can accept in regard to my prodigal is when I do the same things and expect different outcomes.

Lord, I need to relearn how to love without enabling or rescuing. Help me remember to step back and let go of my prodigal, whether I approve of his behavior or not. Flash a neon sign before my eyes that says, "You cannot make anybody change except for yourself." Remind me often that you love my child more than I could ever love him. Forgive me for smothering my prodigal rather than truly loving him. Let me and my prodigal turn to you, the one who is love. As I let go, replace parental guilt with renewed hope.

5

Manipulation

Love can be blind—especially with a prodigal. It's so hard to know if needs and requests are coming from a beloved child or the wily impostor who sometimes takes over. Nobody likes to be taken advantage of, and is that what loving a prodigal is really about? One way to remove the inner tug-of-war is to draw clear boundaries and stick to them. Decide what you will and will not do for your grown child. Spell it out, even if he doesn't agree.

Maybe you decide you'll always give your prodigal food or meet other survival needs, but you'll never give money. Maybe you'll listen to your prodigal but learn to walk away should the conversation become abusive or accusatory. By taking control of your relationship with your prodigal, you may still feel manipulated at times, but your boundaries will stay in place.

Tough Love

*I am afraid that just as Eve was deceived by the
serpent's cunning, your minds may somehow be led
astray from your sincere and pure devotion to Christ.*

2 CORINTHIANS 11:3

Lord, when it comes to my prodigal, I'm a pushover.
Even when I know he's trying to manipulate me, one
flash of that smile I love and I cave in to whatever he's
asking of me. Then I beat myself up for falling for the
same ploy, again and again. Trouble is, it feels like I'm
working with two different people—the child I love and
an impostor who has taken over her mind and body.
In moments of clarity, my child is still the same warm,
good person I've always known. But when the "impostor" takes over, he'll lie, throw tantrums, give the silent
treatment, or blackmail, all for whatever holds my child
hostage. I give in and then feel used, weak, and more
than a little embarrassed.

God, I need your wisdom. When my child's been
hijacked by the impostor, give me a clear mind so I can
act wisely. Help me plan ahead so I know what I can do
for my prodigal and what I will not be pressured into
doing. Keep me from falling into the same manipulative traps, no matter how tempting, no matter how skill-
fully he plays on my emotions. Strengthen my resolve
not to enable or rescue. Help me learn that with a sensi-
ble plan and your help, Lord, I can still love my prodigal
without compromise. That's real tough love.

How Name-Calling Hurts

I prayed, "Hear us, O Lord God, for
we are being mocked."

NEHEMIAH 4:4 TLB

Lord, I raised my prodigal to respect others and be polite. But lately, when she asks for something I can't or won't give, she turns to name-calling. Me, her own parent! The one who gave her life and already supplies more of her demands than I should. At times, the name-calling and profanity stun me—I never would have thought to say such ugly words to my own parents. But the moment I say, "No," the insults, threats, and tantrums begin. At first, I wondered how she ever thought this approach would sway me. Yet I'm ashamed to say I've given in just to stop the barrage of angry labels and profanity. I don't understand my reaction, let alone why she hurts the ones who love her most. I need help.

They say names will never hurt me, but Lord, you know better. You know what it's like to be called foul names, to be mocked and mislabeled. You endured verbal abuse and much more as the Romans tried to manipulate you into admitting guilt. You silently took the abuse and taught us to turn the other cheek when we're mistreated. But I can't stand it without your help, Lord. I need courage to endure, but I also need wisdom to act if verbal abuse becomes physical. Give me strength to resist returning hurtful threats or insults and courage to protect myself if necessary.

Promises, Promises

Let no one deceive you with empty words,
for because of such things God's wrath comes
on those who are disobedient.

EPHESIANS 5:6

My prodigal makes so many promises, Lord. If I'll do what he asks—call in sick for him, replace another broken item, drive miles to pick him up, lend him money— he promises he'll repay, never ask again, take better care of his stuff, or no longer miss work. I want to believe he'll carry through with his promises. But he rarely does. Most of the time, my prodigal is as flaky as a buttermilk biscuit. He was raised to believe that his word is his bond, but as long as he's on the wrong path in life, he doesn't seem to care that he doesn't keep promises. Worse, I never get used to feeling let down each time I allow his manipulative promises to get the best of me.

Lord, I feel betrayed when my child breaks his promises. Help me turn my anger over being "had" into healthy resolve. Let me remember that my child isn't a third grader anymore—he can manage his life as an adult. Keep me from solving his grown-up problems for him; hold me back from saving him from his own failures. Help me let him stumble if he makes mistakes. Teach me, Lord, to love my prodigal with a light touch and long arms.

Who's Crying Wolf?

They will not be sinners, full of lies and deceit.
They will live quietly, in peace, and lie down in
safety, and no one will make them afraid.

Zephaniah 3:13 TLB

Lord, as much as I hate my prodigal's manipulating, I do it too. "If you do that one more time, I'll…" What? Kick him out, call the police, or withhold my money, my time, my love—fill in the blank. I've threatened and then failed to follow through. I've made promises I couldn't keep, whether out of fear or love or lack of backbone. This sick dance has gone on far too long. He sweet-talks and, when I don't give in, he gets mean. I cajole him to straighten out his act and, if he doesn't respond favorably, I get mean. We're guilty of manipulating each other.

Lord, help me step up and stop the manipulating on my part. Threats, whether they come from my prodigal or from me, are like paper tigers, blowing aimlessly in the wind. Help me remember that these tactics keep us from believing anything will change. Give us each the courage to see we're *both* manipulative, acting like the boy who cried wolf. Then, when a real emergency comes up, we might let the wolf stroll in and take the sheep. Help me act first if necessary so that a seed of change can take root. God, give me wisdom to speak truth and only state what I'm actually willing to do. Let me be trustworthy in both word and action so that manipulation has no more place in my life.

Judgment

Black-and-white thinking forces us parents to judge our kids as either good or bad. We know we're supposed to hate the sin and love the sinner, but it all gets mixed up together, reduced to either-or. Either a prodigal is good, or he isn't. She's either with us or against us.

Trouble is, God knows life is more complex than either-or and black-and-white judgments. Love urges us to reject *either-or* and embrace *both-and*. The prodigal is *both* loved *and*, for now, lost. We parents are *both* frustrated *and* still hoping for our children. By adjusting our thinking from shades of gray to living color, parents of prodigals can begin to see a rainbow of possibilities. Try making a both-and list for you and your prodigal and see if colorful sprouts of hope begin to grow.

Choosing Mercy

Judgment without mercy will be shown to anyone who has not been merciful. Mercy triumphs over judgment.

JAMES 2:13

Judging my prodigal seems to hinge on whether I believe he's choosing his path—or it's choosing him. No one says they'd like to be an addict or criminal or a terrible person when they grow up. And we all make bad choices from time to time. Yet with my prodigal, Lord, it's not about occasionally stumbling. He's been driving the wrong way down a one-way street for too long. How do I show mercy without judging? Is he choosing this path? Or is there something more going on?

Only you, Lord, can help me with this delicate balance. No law, rule book, or standard will give me the answers, and all the wisdom of man will not tell me exactly what is right. Let me look to you, the Lord of love, in every situation. If I think I'm showing mercy, and it turns out to be enabling, let me learn and take a step back. If I've been burned one too many times, help me refrain from judgment that writes off my prodigal as a "bad" person. Give me an understanding heart, Lord, one that sees the fear in my prodigal. Help me deal gently, so that when he's ready to head toward home, I can welcome him with loving arms.

Who's Holier?

*Let any one of you who is without sin be
the first to throw a stone at her.*

JOHN 8:7

Lord, I feel so judged. My friends and family appear disgusted that I can't seem to make my prodigal straighten up and fly right. They're weary of hearing me tell about the latest crisis. Fresh out of patience for both of us, they judge my prodigal and me. My child's bad and I'm weak, all because I can't force a change. It hurts when others tell me what they'd do in my moccasins, especially when they've never walked a step in my shoes. "Just kick him out," one says. "He's obviously choosing this life." "You need some tough love," another adds. I find myself either defending my prodigal or else shutting down and never saying another word about it. Being judged is as painful as watching my prodigal stumble.

Lord, can I just cry on your shoulder? Encircle me with your arms and soothe my raw emotions. You know I'm doing my best with a tough situation. You know my intentions, and you know all about my prodigal. Best of all, you love us both more than anyone else can. Dry my tears, Lord, and help me stand tall as I remember that you are the final judge. Those who would throw stones at me are no doubt harboring their own secrets. But they're probably doing their best too. Keep my heart soft, Lord. Let me not grow bitter or resentful against those who would judge my prodigal and me.

New Eyes

Judgment will again be just,
and all the upright will rejoice.

PSALM 94:15 TLB

Lord, in your creation, you've allowed free will. How wonderful that people aren't robots—but this free will also confounds and saddens those of us with prodigals. We parents can't reconcile man's judgment of evil with the precious children we love. Yet I can imagine a day when our understanding more closely matches your perfect judgment. For those with addiction, new treatment methods and laws are beginning to shift away from simple punishment and toward a more merciful approach. Instead of tossing addicts into jail, we're discovering better ways to help them find sobriety and reclaim their lives. This loving approach—offering help without condemnation—is surely closer to what you had in mind.

Lord, I'm optimistic and hopeful that as our ideas about addiction change for the better, so will our attitudes toward addicts of all types. Give me courage to speak this truth to those who are angry or convinced all prodigals are worthless or in need of punishment. Help me advocate for the treatment methods and judgments which address root causes of dysfunction. Give me new eyes to see that love—even tough love—can solve these problems in ways that punishment never will. Most of all, let me accept others the way you do—right where they are, right now.

Shut My Mouth

"Learn to be wise," he said, "and develop good judgment and common sense! I cannot overemphasize this point."

Proverbs 4:5 TLB

Sometimes, Lord, my judgment isn't the best. In this crazy situation with my prodigal, I don't always use common sense. Even though my prodigal's the one who's lost the possession, the opportunity, or the job, I take it upon myself to fix, cover up, or explain away his poor choices. If I'm honest, I see that one reason I make these mistakes in judgment is that I want whatever is in danger more than my prodigal wants it. I know how hard it will be to find money to replace stuff, to search for opportunities that might lead to a better life, to get another job. That's why I rush to keep the status quo. That's why I'm willing to live a lie.

Lord, only you can help me out of this crazy pit. I love my prodigal, but I *am not* my prodigal. Give me courage to face my tendency to protect my child and prevent me from meddling in his life. Help me learn to stand back and lovingly allow him to stumble if necessary. Keep reminding me that only Jesus Christ can truly change people—and they must want to change. Stand me on my feet, tie my hands, tape shut my mouth—Lord, do whatever it takes to hold me back. Then maybe my prodigal will learn to be wise on his own.

7

Faith

To a parent of a prodigal, it may often seem as if God's on vacation. That maybe the "Big Guy Upstairs" is just too busy to fix every wayward kid who comes along. We know it's not true, but during trying times with our prodigals, our faith can feel too small, like trying to pull on tight pants that won't zip up no matter what we do. Our faith gets crammed into skinny jeans that won't let us breathe and make us feel like we're wearing a boa constrictor.

To keep faith growing, peel off those uncomfortable pants and dig into the Bible. Grab your favorite translation and read or listen to Scripture on a regular basis. Focus on a few hopeful verses and then test them—that is, apply them to your life. After a while, instead of trying to squeeze faith into your messy parent life, you'll be able to step into a faith that can take you anywhere God sends you.

Baby Steps

If you had faith even as small as a tiny mustard seed, you could say to this mountain, "Move!" and it would go far away. Nothing would be impossible.

MATTHEW 17:20 TLB

Lord, you know my three sons have been wandering as addicted prodigals for years now. At first I'd hoped it was a stage they'd grow out of and prayed for them to return to the straight and narrow way. They didn't, yet my faith, although sometimes shaky, survived. Then, as they became adults and years turned to decades, I had to fight to keep what little faith I could. You saw as my husband and I tried forcing our sons to meetings, treatment programs, and 12-step groups, but they kept walking away, kept digging in to hard-core substance abuse. My faith shrank to microscopic size, as the deliverance or healing I craved from you didn't come.

Lord, I thank you for my faith—as teensy as it is. My hopes felt smaller than a mustard seed when I only wanted you to heal my boys miraculously. Now I see how much more abundant life in you can be as I take baby steps. Faith still sometimes flickers in my heart, but now it's growing again. It's growing because I've stopped basing my faith on the cure that I wanted but didn't receive. The day I started believing in your promises of compassion, mercy, grace, and love, my faith soared.

Continue showing me how to grow my faith as I press closer to you. Let me trust you for faith that grows so much that even my wayward sons will marvel—and maybe even surrender their lives to you too.

God Is Faithful

Let love and faithfulness never leave you;
bind them around your neck,
write them on the tablet of your heart.

PROVERBS 3:3

At times I'm so tempted to give up, Lord. My prodigal breaks his promises as if they were dry twigs. Why, then, should I do everything I say I will do? When my prodigal is unreliable or lets me down, I feel like giving him a dose of his own medicine. I know it's not easy to stop an addiction or any wrong behavior, but it's difficult to walk the straight and narrow path too.

I'm grateful for your faithfulness. When my prodigal breaks a promise and I feel hurt, help me remember that you alone, Lord God, are righteous. You alone can judge the world. Whether we are saints or sinners, no one is perfect except you. Help me remember that although my prodigal can be unreliable, you are faithful and will never let me down. Your promises endure forever.

Instant Miracles

Jesus said to her, "Woman, you have great
faith! Your request is granted." And her
daughter was healed at that moment.

MATTHEW 15:28

When I got an Instant Pot for a gift, Lord—one of those
fancy, cook-everything-in-a-snap pressure cookers—it
reminded me of stories in the Bible where Jesus healed
folks on the spot. A leper was cleansed, a blind man saw,
a withered hand became strong. Most of the healings
were instant miracles. I don't doubt the healings, but
the stories make me long for an instant miracle for my
prodigal. I don't know if my faith is too small or if one
of us has not done something necessary. While I know
it's wrong to reduce your healing powers to a formula of
some kind, my questions keep building. Why, Lord, do
those of us with prodigals seem to wait forever?

The moment I ask this, Lord, I hear you asking Job where
he was when you created the world.[1] While you're a big
enough God to welcome my questions, your knowledge is also so vast that my puny mind can never grasp
your reasoning. Instead of giving me instant solutions,
give me a heart of gratitude. Help me see the positive
side as I deal with my prodigal child. Help me cultivate
compassion, kindness, and love. Grow my faith so I can
become as patient with my child as you are with me.

Tempted to Run

*No temptation has overtaken you that is not
common to man. God is faithful, and he will
not let you be tempted beyond your strength, but
with the temptation will also provide the way
of escape, that you may be able to endure it.*

1 CORINTHIANS 10:13 RSV

My prodigal did it again, Lord. She talked me into believing that this time things would be different. Sure, she's disappointed me before, but this time I wanted—no, needed—to believe her. My prodigal has cried wolf too many times to count, but I wanted to give her the benefit of the doubt. Give her one more chance. I held up my end of the bargain, but my prodigal left me holding the bag—a bag full of dashed hopes. This time, Lord, disappointment tastes even more bitter than usual. I'm so far down, I wish I could escape, just run away to some desert island.

All I can do is hold on to you for dear life. Thank you, Lord, for being the same loving God no matter how I feel or what I do. Your faithfulness keeps me from sinking when my resolve turns to jelly. Your compassion brings me up for air like a mother whale guides her calf to the surface to breathe. Your faithfulness helps me keep swimming toward hope, and if my faith isn't big enough, you keep me floating in the warm sea of your love. When I'm disappointed, don't let me become bitter. Instead, help me see your way of escape.

8

Hope

For us parents of prodigals, hope is like water—necessary for life. Faith is a well that helps us keep hope alive, but often we feel as if we walk a lonely highway, a road with endless switchbacks and blistering sun. As we wander in a barren desert, hope evaporates, leaving us sunburnt and parched.

To quench this desperate thirst for hope, God places an oasis in our lives called Gratitude. In the middle of nowhere, a lush, green garden of gratefulness awaits. As the book of Isaiah says, "Ho! Every one who thirsts, come to the waters" (55:1 NASB). At times we might worry that this Gratitude is only a mirage, but we keep slogging across burning sand. Finally, we sink down at the water's edge, thanking God for his protection. As we slake our thirst with gratitude, our wilted hope perks up and begins to grow.

In the Deep

I am utterly helpless, without any hope.

JOB 6:13 TLB

He got clean for a while, Lord, but then he relapsed. He came back to us, but now he's gone again. I had such high hopes this time, but all it did was give me more distance to fall. Now I'm so far down, my soul feels turned inside out. It was foolish to put all my hopes into one basket, but I did. And now my prodigal is back to the old ways, but I can't seem to swim back to hope. I feel like someone wrapped in chains who's been pitched overboard into a deep black sea. Why hope if I'm just going to end up in the abyss? I can't hold my breath one more second, Lord, and I'm sinking fast. Help!

Lord, when I cry out to you, I open my eyes. There you are, swimming right beside me. You don't give me a lecture about staying positive, and you don't chide me for losing hope. No. I wish you'd just pluck me out of the depths and drop me onto dry land, but instead, you show me a way to breathe underwater. Lord, help me see the good in my prodigal, even when we're both stranded at sea. Help me stop obsessing about his progress. Guide me to focus on the changes *I* need to make in order to survive this tempest. Thank you that you breathe new hope into me.

Keeping Hope Alive

Hope does not put us to shame, because God's love has been poured out into our hearts through the Holy Spirit, who has been given to us.

In wartime, the hope of a reunion with deployed soldiers keeps families going. I feel like I'm enduring the same kind of waiting. If my prodigal acts selfishly or disregards the morals we taught him, my hopes for recovery start to dim. Even worse, if I make excuses for my prodigal, justify his actions, or cover up his misdeeds, then I'm not innocent either. Times like those, I feel ashamed—and disappointed in myself.

When my emotions get tangled, help me hope in you, Lord. Thank you for the assurance that hope *won't* be put to shame and *can't* disappoint. Lord, you aren't ashamed of me, so how can I be ashamed of my prodigal? Yes, sin has consequences. But help me remember that even when we go the wrong way, you keep hope for all your children burning brightly. Help me leave a candle burning in the window in hopes that my prodigal will come sailing home soon.

Hope's Empty Plate

Remember your word to your servant,
for you have given me hope.

Psalm 119:49

I've been through so much with my prodigal that I can almost see it coming. He talks about recovery for a day or a week, and I delight in the way he acts like the wonderful person he was before he strayed. If he says he'll be home for dinner, he shows up on time. But then things change, sometimes so subtly that I miss the signs. His open and honest manner becomes secretive. Now, instead of letting us know of his comings and goings, he abruptly disappears. His place at the dinner table remains empty. And before I know it, the deadly cycle starts over again. Those are the times when my prodigal's behavior threatens to pull the plug on my hope. How can I continue to hope when Dr. Jekyll keeps turning into Mr. Hyde?

The answer, Lord, lies only with you. Hope can stay alive if I trust you and your Word. Over and over in Scripture, Lord, you reassure me. You promise never to leave me. You protect me and guide my every step. Your love for my prodigal and me is forever. With you, nothing is impossible. I want to see my prodigal as you do, Lord, full of hope for his healing, full of love for your child and mine. Help me see that hope is not really made of circumstances that shift direction like the wind. Fill me with the kind of hope that only your Holy Spirit can deliver—a hope that sees past our failings, looks behind the masks we wear, and dares to grow even when disappointment catches us off guard. Lord, I want the kind of hope that sees beyond the empty dinner plate.

Gardens of Hope

*"I know the plans I have for you," declares
the Lord, "plans to prosper you and not to harm
you, plans to give you hope and a future."*

JEREMIAH 29:11

Here in the Pacific Northwest, the winter landscape looks dead and brown. Life with my prodigal often feels the same way—a long winter of bare branches and wilted remains of flowers and shrubs. Biting wind and cold rain greet me if I venture outside, and it's nearly impossible to imagine the warmth and beauty of last year's blooms. Some days I don't even want to get out of bed. Why bother when my grown child's behavior is only apt to hurt me again?

But by February, Lord, you cause pink, purple, and white crocuses to poke their little heads out of the frozen ground. Your creation's cheery colors offer new hope at a time when mine is barely clinging to life. The promise of spring reawakens my fading hope for a future with my prodigal, a future that will prosper us in ways that you design. Even though it's hard to keep waiting for winter to be over, each spring bloom reminds me that the seasons and cycles of life are all a part of your plan. Help me haul myself out of bed today, Lord, and wrap me in the hope of a future as beautiful as the first blooms of spring.

9

Forgiveness

You've forgiven your prodigal for hurting you, tarnishing the family's reputation, taking advantage of your generosity, or breaking your heart. You don't intend to think of your prodigal as 100 percent guilty while you're completely innocent, but sometimes the situation does appear lopsided. It may look as if you should do all the forgiving—but look again.

Healthy relationships need communication, and communication needs honesty. Are there areas with your prodigal where you've held back your honest feelings? Places where you've wavered on set boundaries, caved when you promised you'd stand firm? Have you lost your temper, thrown out sarcasm, or judged unfairly? Confess these sins to God and fortify your plan of action for the next time. And someday, when the time is right, ask your prodigal for forgiveness too.

A Key to Forgiveness

He got up and went to his father. But while he
was still a long way off, his father saw him and
was filled with compassion for him; he ran to his
son, threw his arms around him and kissed him.

Luke 15:20

When my prodigal does or says hurtful things, pain digs a hole in me. Even if I know my child really doesn't mean it, saying or doing things to manipulate me or make me angry just causes a deeper rift between us. I confess that I tend to want to hurt him back or to let loose the anger that has been growing in me as he refuses to come back to the ways our family teaches him to honor. Those times, love for my child feels like a burned-out shell, and his behavior strands him in a land of no return. I don't know how I can ever forgive.

Thank you, Lord, for the story of the prodigal son, which fills me with hope that my prodigal and I can find the road to forgiveness. Remind me that the path that leads to home doesn't require me being a doormat, that I needn't tolerate insults or sinful behavior. Help me remember that you are more merciful than an angry old guy throwing lightning bolts—but that you hate sin too. Help me balance compassion and consequences with my prodigal, always keeping in mind that you, Lord, want what's best for all of us. Soften my heart and keep me willing to take the first step toward forgiveness. When conflict arises, show me how to respond to my child with courage and wisdom.

No Grudges

When you are praying, first forgive anyone you
are holding a grudge against, so that your Father
in heaven will forgive you your sins too.

MARK 11:25 TLB

When the crisis dies down, anger at my prodigal some-times stays strong. Whether I've been duped into enabling or outright lied to, it's hard to shake the righ-teous indignation I feel knowing my own child has betrayed our family's values. How could he hurt us that way? Why is he so ungrateful for all the help we give him? He doesn't deserve our love and loyalty. Although I haven't disowned my wayward prodigal, I admit I've felt like doing so. It's hard not to have a chip on my shoulder.

Yet, Father, when I set aside my wounded feelings, I see that your children hurt you too. Come to think of it, we all fall short. Time after time, you became mad as all get-out at the Israelites who wandered in the desert. Then, as now, nobody deserves anything but your wrath. But instead, you show mercy, graciously forgiving us for all manner of mistakes. Let me remember that you aren't a God of grudges—time after time you've wiped the slate clean for me. Father, help me let go of angry grudges and, instead, practice merciful forgiveness with my prodigal and everyone I meet.

Throwing Stones

*You are a God of forgiveness, always ready
to pardon, gracious and merciful, slow to
become angry, and full of love and mercy.*

NEHEMIAH 9:17 TLB

Lord, when my prodigal pushes me past my breaking point, it's hard not to fight back. If she calls me names, I can barely keep from using words as a weapon too. If she takes something without permission and then doesn't make it right or fails to meet obligations, sarcasm floods out of me. For an angry moment, I want my prodigal to hurt as badly as I hurt. I pick up some smooth stones, flinging out hurtful labels like "addict," "ne'er-do-well," "slacker," "deadbeat," "loser." Although I know it only feeds my thirst for revenge, throwing stones gives me a twisted satisfaction. But I not only further damage my relationship with my grown child—I feel far away from you, God.

Lord, when I'm hurt, take away my tendency to want to get even. Remind me that this prodigal is still my child, even though she's an adult, and I love her. Let me remember that sarcasm hurts too. If she, or anyone else, acts like a playground bully, fill me with the love and mercy I need to put down the stones and forgive.

Forgiving Times Infinity

Peter came to Jesus and asked, "Lord, how many times shall I forgive my brother or sister who sins against me? Up to seven times?" Jesus answered, "I tell you, not seven times, but seventy-seven times."

MATTHEW 18:21-22

God, I'm sick of this whole dance. My prodigal goofs up. Hurt and anger get all mixed up with my love for my child. He apologizes. I forgive. Then it all starts over again. Some days I think it might be easier to just cut the cord and completely end my relationship with my grown child. I wouldn't have to watch his sick dance, and he'd never again come crawling back with his promise to be better. I wouldn't have to forgive him for his behavior, and he'd stop feeling nagged and misunderstood. The world would see how wrong he is, and everyone would know how much I've been hurt.

Who am I kidding, Lord? As sick as I am of the situation, I don't want to stop hoping my prodigal will turn around. Even if I'm forced to sever our physical relationship, I could never cut my prodigal out of my heart. And martyrdom sounds lonely too. Father, as I step onto the dance floor, help me hold on to you, not self-pity. Lead me in making sure that love—for you, my prodigal, my family, myself—takes center stage every day, in every way. Help me remember that my prodigal is tired of the dance too. Let me forgive him in love, as many times as it takes, until at last my prodigal comes waltzing home.

10

Change

Parents of prodigals expect sudden changes. Every day we walk on eggshells and wait for the other shoe to drop. When our prodigal vows to change but fails, we say, "Talk is cheap. Show me." And sometimes, without meaning to, we withhold trust, encouragement, and even love *until* he changes.

But that's not how God loves us. Again and again, God forgives us, shows us compassion, and loves us when we don't deserve it. God risks being rejected, even hurt, by humans who promise to do better but then slide back into the same old sins. God accepts us anyway, while we are still covered in muddy mistakes. He doesn't love us once we've changed. Instead, God loves us so that we *can* change. Embracing your muddy prodigal with godly love just might help him take the first step toward home.

Stand Back

The Lord, the God of Israel says: Even yet, if you quit your evil ways, I will let you stay in your own land.

Jeremiah 7:3 tlb

When my prodigal was little, if his pants grew soggy, I changed them. As his parent, I controlled when he ate, napped, and played. Now that my child is grown, I can still see clearly where he needs to change. But he isn't willing. Lord, in my desperation for his life to change, I've prayed, begged, and even tried to bargain. *If you'll heal my prodigal,* I've prayed, *I'll change for the better. I'll never ask anything again. I'll be good—I promise!* The problem is, as much as you desire to see my prodigal whole, you know that healing must come from within. The healing-by-proxy that I'm pleading for leaves out an important truth: We cannot change anyone except ourselves.

Lord, heal my heart. Your concept of change is so hard for me to accept. Teach me to let go of the urge to "help" my prodigal change and, instead, let me simply love him. Shift my prayers away from nagging or bargaining and toward gratitude and praise. Quiet the anxious thoughts that lead me to try to change my prodigal. Let me dwell on your peace to put my mind at ease. Help me stand back and concentrate on the only thing in this life I can change: myself.

PRAYERS *for* PARENTS *of* PRODIGALS

Stay in Your Lane

Repent, then, and turn to God, so that
your sins may be wiped out, that times of
refreshing may come from the Lord.

ACTS 3:19

Some days I get so bound up with worry, hurt, and anger that I don't make time for you, Lord. Morning quiet time gets bumped. Running errands for my prodigal or fixing his problems somehow sucks away my plans for devotions, prayers, or meditations. Even when I do make time to spend with you, Lord, oftentimes I'm a blubbering mess of tears and pain. I feel as if I'm living two lives—my own and that of my prodigal child. I attend to my grown child's life more than my own. And many times I don't manage any of our problems very well.

Lord, I see how much I miss you when I skip prayer time. I desperately need refreshment, a fresh start to refocus my life. Help me allow my prodigal to tend to his life like the adult he's become. Give me strength to make regular time for you, that I may put on my spiritual armor each day. Give me the courage to stay in my own lane and admit and correct my course when I start to drift back into old habits. Lord, let your time of refreshing wash over me, with the assurance that you will be with my prodigal everywhere he goes.

The Better Path

Woe to you, teachers of the law and Pharisees, you hypocrites! You give a tenth of your spices—mint, dill and cumin. But you have neglected the more important matters of the law—justice, mercy and faithfulness. You should have practiced the latter, without neglecting the former.

MATTHEW 23:23

Change is scary, Lord; I get that. Still, I want my prodigal to stop fighting me and return to the sweet, caring person she once was. Why do I need to change? I don't steal or cheat or use people. I don't break promises or lie to my loved ones. *I'm* doing just fine. My prodigal has hurt me and the rest of the family by her actions and words. She's walked away from the rules we live by and neglected to live up to our standards. I can't put up with what she's doing—it's not right. When she's ready to change, we'll talk.

Lord, help me do and say what's right without completely shutting out my prodigal. In my hurt and grief, I often concentrate too much on justice and not enough upon mercy. Even if my prodigal and I must be apart due to violence or uncontrolled anger, teach me to see her through your compassion. Let me flee from all forms of hypocrisy and reroute my thoughts away from strict adherence to the law and more toward the grace you offer each of us. Prevent me from judging my prodigal without compassion; show me that mercy is not the same as weakness. Help me see that as scary as change can be, I can become kinder, more grace filled, and loving toward my prodigal while still resisting evil.

Shine Bright

Jesus Christ is the same yesterday and today and forever.

HEBREWS 13:8

If and when my prodigal starts for home, I know, Lord, that a lot will have to change. We'll need to find new ways of talking to each other and, even more importantly, new ways of listening to each other. If I cling to old ways, I'll risk falling back into poor habits or missing opportunities to reconnect with my prodigal. Who knows? If he sees me working to change, he may be motivated to work on our relationship too. And even if my child stays far off, I can still change so that I might see with eyes of compassion, hear with ears of mercy, and speak with a voice of kindness. In this world change comes whether I'm ready or not. No matter what, I want to change so that I lean on you more and more. You are *always* the Lord of creation.

Lord, free me from thinking I can never change unless my prodigal comes home. I praise you that I can trust you with the changes in both my life and my prodigal's life. Thank you for your steadfast assurance that you are the same yesterday, today, and forever—through you I have courage to face whatever happens. Keep my heart filled with love for you and my prodigal, preserve my hope in your goodness, comfort me when changes are hard. Let me shine bright for Jesus so that my prodigal knows he is loved today, tomorrow, and forever.

11

Anger

Whether you're a yeller, a brooder, or you just grow depressed, it's hard to control anger that erupts over a prodigal's behavior. The way your child should go is as plain as the nose on your face—but that kid keeps going the opposite direction. It's hard not to stay mad—at your prodigal, at the world. And getting angry without sinning? Even harder.

So what *can* you do to control anger? The old "count to ten" trick is worth a try. Forcing yourself to wait before you express anger can calm you down if you're impulsive and help you discover if your strong feelings are necessary. If you're more of a grudge holder, step up your forgiveness. Forgiving helps you release those negative feelings. And don't forget your sense of humor. Finding the funny in even the most serious of situations can help you keep your circumstances in perspective and your temper in check.

Seeing Red, Offering Grace

In your anger do not sin.

EPHESIANS 4:26

Wow, Lord. So often I'm mad at my prodigal for so many things. My blood boils every time she asks me to call in when she misses work. I loathe the way she ignores opportunities in order to pursue her own selfish needs or neglects the people who love her. I see red when I think of how her behavior costs me time, money, and patience. Not to mention the negative shadow all this casts on the rest of us! Even my closest friends don't always understand about our prodigal problem, which makes it even more maddening. At times, Lord, my prodigal gets me so het up I can't see straight. And I'm supposed to get mad but not sin? Sounds impossible.

Father, without you by my side, I guess it *is* impossible. True, I have plenty to be mad about—it's human to feel hurt and angry when trust is violated, when promises are broken, when boundaries have been crossed. Yet when I'm about to blow my stack, help me slow down. Remind me first to take a deep breath and then let it out. If need be, I can count to ten. Let me ask myself if it's worth working myself up into a lather. God, refocus my anger away from nitpicking or haranguing and back to hating the sin but loving the sinner. Yes, a prodigal can really get under a parent's skin, but anger doesn't have to be toxic. When I'm seeing red, Lord, teach me to offer grace instead.

Poison Arrows

My dear brothers and sisters, take note of this: Everyone should be quick to listen, slow to speak and slow to become angry.

JAMES 1:19

When I'm angry, sarcastic barbs sit on my tongue like poisoned arrows, ready to aim for my prodigal's weakest place. In the heat of the moment, it's tempting to blurt out everything I've been thinking. *You're nothing but a… You did it again, didn't you? Why won't you get help?* If he's failed, I point it out and rub it in. Then my prodigal uses words to hurt me, so I hurt back. He hurls back insults and denies he has a problem. As long as he won't change, everything I say just goes in one ear and out the other anyway. In anger, I think, *My prodigal won't listen to me, so why should I listen to him?*

But once my anger dies down, I feel awful, Lord. Do I really have to say every word that comes to mind? Help me see that by not listening to my child, I'm doing far more than simply dismissing his choices. I'm dismissing him. Help me learn that better communication not only keeps us from ending up in shouting matches, but it can also help me understand my prodigal and show him he is loved. Remind me that some words are better left unsaid, but that loving speech can help mend injured egos and broken hearts. Lord, before I shoot poison arrows of anger, teach me to think before I speak, to ask myself: *Are my words a blessing? Are they full of truth and peace? Am I speaking what is good or what is evil?* I pray my prodigal will see that no matter how mad I get, my love for him is forever.

Time-Out

O Lord, don't punish me while you are angry!

PSALM 38:1 TLB

Before my prodigal was born, I learned that parents shouldn't discipline while they are angry. But after she grew into a typical toddler, I saw how tough it can be to separate discipline from emotions. Now, as an adult, my prodigal doesn't have to obey me at all. But when she heads even farther down a dangerous or destructive path, it's harder than ever to keep my anger at bay. It's excruciating to hold my tongue—especially when *her* temper seems to flare at every trivial thing. *She ought to know better*, I think. *Why doesn't she ever learn?* My own irritation can quickly ignite and, before I know it, we're both as full of rage as tantrum-throwing two-year-olds. The worst part is that, in anger, we've each said hurtful words we didn't mean.

Lord, I'm thankful that you are slow to anger. If you punished us as we deserve, nobody would stand. Instead, thanks to Jesus, we receive love instead of punishment, and even when we should reap what we sow, his sacrifice covers our sins. Lord, when I'm mad at my prodigal, help me take the high road. Give me strength to wait until I'm calm to discuss consequences with my prodigal. Help me neither to bribe nor to threaten, but to reason with my child with a level head and a steely resolve. You, Lord, are always the same. Let me model consistency to my prodigal, and if I'm so mad I can't be mature with her, nudge me to take a time-out so I can seek your wisdom until I can process my anger and relate to my child in love once more.

Shake It Off

Do not repay evil with evil or insult with insult.
On the contrary, repay evil with blessing,
because to this you were called so that
you may inherit a blessing.

1 PETER 3:9

Once, a good Christian woman heard about my three boys' struggles with addiction and remarked, "You obviously didn't raise them right." Lord, that was years ago, and it still stings. When others make hurtful comments, my emotions rush to the surface. I'm hurt, sad, and mad all at once, and getting even feels like an itch I really want to scratch. I don't exactly fantasize about wringing that woman's neck, but I'm quick to judge her and wish I could repay her with a snappy comeback. If *I* say something negative about my prodigal, it's one thing. But let somebody else run him down, and I turn into a mother grizzly bear. A very angry mother grizzly.

But Lord, revenge isn't how you operate. Even though in ancient times it was "eye for eye,"[2] Jesus commands us to bless and not curse. Although turning the other cheek and blessing that lady doesn't scratch my get-even itch, help me do it for you. Help me learn that when I return insult for insult, a bad situation only gets worse. Nursing a grudge only hurts me. Show me how to shake off the words of those who don't understand what it's like to have a prodigal, Lord. I'm ready to inherit a blessing.

Enabling

Gymnasts tumble every which way but still maintain balance. Similarly, our emotions often twist and toss about as parents of prodigals. Each new crisis and heartbreak challenges us to endure the ordeal while keeping good posture, maintaining focus, and even landing on our feet. The most difficult move of all is to love the prodigal without enabling.

To make matters more complicated, not everyone agrees on what constitutes enabling. Some argue that any support is enabling. Others stop at giving food or shelter. No matter where helping ends and enabling begins in your mind, stay close to God as you grapple with prodigal requests. Endeavor to live as Jesus commands: "Love the Lord your God with all your heart and with all your soul and with all your mind," and, "Love your neighbor as yourself" (Matthew 22:37,39). If you do these things, you're sure to stick the landing of love.

Overhelping Enabler

God is our refuge and strength,
a very present help in trouble.

PSALM 46:1 RSV

I'm an excellent helper, Lord. When a job needs volunteers, I almost always raise my hand. It feels right to assist others, especially if they are down on their luck. Jesus commands us to love our neighbor as ourselves, and that's how I live. Trouble is, helping takes on a whole new meaning when the other person is down on their luck *and* happens to be my own offspring. When my prodigal needs any sort of help, it's next to impossible for me not to spring into action to solve his problem. I help my prodigal, and the short-term problem is solved. But the prodigal stays childlike—and I get labeled an *enabler*.

Lord, help me set up firm boundaries with my prodigal. Let me ask myself if the need is something he could take care of on his own. By helping, am I keeping my prodigal from experiencing the consequences any adult should face due to negligence or poor planning? Am I giving my prodigal a handout or a hand up? Lord, if I step over the line of helper and into enabler territory, pull me back so my prodigal can grow into his adult role. Comfort me if consequences are painful but necessary. Lord, let me show my prodigal the better path by loving him but allowing him to find you as his very present help in times of trouble.

Wise Steps

Do not be wise in your own eyes;
fear the LORD and shun evil.

PROVERBS 3:7

So often when I help my prodigal, I tell myself that she couldn't do it on her own. When she was little, she clutched my fingers to steady herself. But she gained as much strength and balance from falling down as she did from taking steps. Now *I'm* the one holding on. Instead of teaching my prodigal to take the steps she needs to be independent, I assume she either can't or won't learn what needs doing. Every time I swoop down to save the day, I'm holding her back. By refusing to allow her to fall on her way to managing her life effectively, I ensure my job as chief enabler will be secure.

Lord, forgive me for underestimating my prodigal's abilities. My enabling prevents her from flying. By helping when I should be nudging her out of the nest, I cripple her future. Grant me the self-control I need to break the enabling habit. Let me not lean on my own understanding or keep my prodigal from believing in her abilities. Show me that enabling, at its root, assumes that I'm wise in my own eyes. Lord, give both of us the courage we need to walk your path. Thank you that we can look to you every moment as you direct our steps.

Loving Myself

You, then, who teach others, do you not teach yourself?

ROMANS 2:21

I admit it. I'm a people pleaser. I go to great lengths to help, give of my time, and be there for others. I want everyone—including my prodigal—to feel happy and satisfied. If my prodigal needs something done at the last moment, I rush to make sure it happens on time. If he needs help in the middle of the night, the middle of the movie, the middle of my morning coffee, I drop everything and go. People are pleased all right. The only person on the verge of falling apart is me.

Lord, by continually pleasing people, I confess that I neglect my own health and needs. I go out of my way for others, including my prodigal, without taking care of my own body, mind, and spirit. Let me think twice before loading one more task on my overloaded plate. Help me learn that it's okay if I pass on family or community projects—those without prodigals may not understand how heavy the burden can be. Teach me to help others without ignoring my own needs, to say that dreaded word, "No." Let me lean on you, Lord, taking time to renew and refresh my spiritual life. With your help, I will turn away from being a people pleaser and instead give myself the same loving care I've given to others.

Help the Helper

Go and learn what this means, "I desire mercy, and not sacrifice." For I came not to call the righteous, but sinners.

Matthew 9:13 rsv

Lord, I love helping people. But I have a hard time accepting help. Most of the time I'm maxed out, rushing around and trying to be everything to everybody. I cook, clean, drive, and volunteer. I "do it all" with a smile on my face, but inside, I'm fuming. My prodigal is so used to my super-parent routine that he doesn't understand why I feel overwhelmed. Maybe he even believes I *like* doing everything. If he steps up and offers help, I brush him off, saying, "Oh no, I can handle it." If he shrugs and says, "Okay," I might even slam some doors, just to be sure he knows what a sacrifice I'm making for him.

Lord, you desire mercy, not sacrifice—especially sacrifice that's offered with self-pity or a grudge. If I feel taken advantage of, let me learn to say no. Help me lay aside the pride that says I must be able to do it all, and let me learn that accepting help is not weakness but strength. With your strength, Lord, I don't need others' praise for my help. I can learn better self-care and show my prodigal that helping others in a spirit of giving is more pleasing than help given with conditions. Lord, I want to trade in my super-parent suit—it doesn't fit me anymore—and instead put on the kinds of behavior I want to see in my prodigal.

Unsolicited Advice

Aprodigal in the family makes almost everyone squirm. Some people offer suggestions out of love or from experience, but most give unsolicited advice to help themselves feel better. Handing out solutions—however pat or inappropriate—eases that uncomfortable feeling for the advice giver. But we parents often feel worse than before.

What should our response be? To cope with the "If I were you" kind of advice, first consider the source. Is this someone with authority or experience? If not, be polite. "I'll pray about it" and "That's an interesting idea" are examples of polite responses that don't give away your power. Most of the time, it's pointless to try to educate the advice giver or change their views. But if the advice goes against your values, you can say, "Thanks, but I'm not going to do that." That's being assertive, not aggressive.

Dirty Laundry

*May your unfailing love come to me, L*ORD,
your salvation, according to your promise;
then I can answer anyone who taunts me,
for I trust in your word.

PSALM 119:41-42

I used to blab about our prodigal challenges to anyone who'd listen. "You won't believe what he did this time," I'd say, sharing all my family's dirty laundry with friends and acquaintances. My heart was full to bursting with the grief, pain, and uncertainty that comes with parenting a prodigal, and telling others about our pain helped me soldier on. At least I thought so—until an avalanche of advice hit me. When well-meaning friends and family weighed in, I was surprised and unprepared for the cut-and-dried answers. "Kick him out." "Cut him off." "Show him tough love." As if it were that simple. The worst suggestions often come from those who don't have a clue what I'm dealing with. All the advice sounds to me more like criticism than help. It's enough to make me vow never to say another word about my prodigal.

Father, I don't want to burden others with my story, especially if I'm not willing to take the advice they offer. When I pour out my heart about my prodigal, people don't always understand that I need comfort, not a lecture. Fill me with your love, Lord, that I might think twice before I share my family's problems with anyone else but you. Help me look to you for comfort when advice feels more like a put-down. Remind me that those not walking in my shoes can never understand what it's like and give me grace to be kind to those who insist they have all the answers. Teach me that I don't have to broadcast my problems to the world. Help me choose not to take personally the unhelpful suggestions, but keep me open to your wisdom, your truth, your love.

Prayer Chains

A gossip goes around spreading rumors, while
a trustworthy man tries to quiet them.

Proverbs 11:13 TLB

Of course I believe in the power of prayer, but sometimes I'm tempted to give more information than my prayer partners need—just so the situation with my prodigal receives more earnest prayers. "Pray for my prodigal" sounds less interesting than "Pray my prodigal stops getting into fistfights with his brother like he did last night." When it comes to praying for my prodigal, sometimes my prayer requests start to sound like gossip. At times, yes, my heart is so hurt and full of pain that I can't contain my anguish. But if I'm giving details in the name of prayer that tempt others to judge or condemn my prodigal, my family, and me, how am I helping? In dysfunctional families like ours, the unwritten rule is *Don't talk; don't tell.* Sharing some of our struggle, even as a prayer request, helps me overcome that harmful and oppressive "rule." Yet I hate being isolated due to my prodigal's behavior. I feel so backed into a corner. I need help.

Lord, show me the right balance when I ask for prayers for me and my prodigal. Help me consider the information I give with a prayer request and ask myself what the people praying really need to know. But I don't want to be stranded in a dark closet either. Please send me one trustworthy confidant—a counselor or friend—who can listen when I need to talk, who can keep my confidences and pray with me without broadcasting my problems. Teach me, Lord, to enter my prayer closet diligently as I learn to cast all my cares upon you.

When the Time Is Right

Timely advice is as lovely as gold apples in a silver basket.

Proverbs 25:11 TLB

From year to year I read the same scriptures, hear the same advice concerning my prodigal, and talk about possible solutions again and again. Yet nothing sinks in until, *wham*—suddenly it all makes sense. What has flown under my radar now seems timely and important. For a long while I've known how to stop enabling, for instance, but the necessary steps never felt feasible before. Likewise, I've constantly told my prodigal he must get back on track, but until the time is right, I'm just speaking into a vacuum. The harder I try to force him to "get it," the less he seems inclined to try. And until I am ready to change my pattern of enabling, all the advice in the world is empty chatter. Meanwhile, I must stay alert.

Lord, I don't want to be asleep when your timing arrives. Although it's hard to wait, and advice feels repetitious, help me prepare for the moment when change is ripe. Just as tender bulbs wait in the dark, cold ground, let green shoots of new life stir within my prodigal and me. Keep us looking toward healing, believing in your promises, cultivating hope for a better tomorrow. Transform us as we renew our minds to eagerly await our springtime, always thankful for your perfect timing.

You're Not Alone

Let the message of Christ dwell among you richly
as you teach and admonish one another with all
wisdom through psalms, hymns, and songs from the
Spirit, singing to God with gratitude in your hearts.

COLOSSIANS 3:16

I remember that one Sunday when a small group of women huddled in the church narthex, comforting a member whose prodigal was in crisis. As they took turns trying to soothe her by offering advice, she just sobbed harder. "I can't do this," she lamented. The women encircled this woman with hugs, love, and their best advice. But the only thing that seemed to help her was another woman's simple statement: "You aren't alone." Although the love and hugs were wonderful, knowing that she wasn't alone on this often lonely and heartbreaking road helped in a way nothing else could. Before they ended with prayers and more hugs, they all chanted, "You're not alone." She wiped her tears and smiled.

Lord, help me remember that the best advice in the world can't compare with your way of comforting a grieving parent's heart. The more I keep Jesus' message front and center, the easier it will be to give comfort to others with prodigals and also to receive the comfort that arises when I help others. Thank you for your Spirit, who lifts us with songs and times of worship and inspires us to sing to you, Father, in gratitude. When I feel isolated, help me remember that you are always with me. I may endure the pain that comes from parenting a prodigal, but I thank you that I am never alone.

14

Answers

The one answer we long for is our prodigals' return home. We want our prodigals to change, and we want it now. Sobriety, healing, a godly life—all these things seem to hinge on that single answer to prayer. Our hopes soar when the prodigal makes a tiny bit of progress. Hopes crash each time there's a relapse or the prodigal runs farther away. We read our Bibles in search of wisdom that will draw our prodigals back to us.

But the Scriptures also overflow with people disappointed by answers that didn't look the way they desired or come as quickly as they hoped. All Nehemiah's people had been weeping as they listened to the words of the Law. This would be miserable news if the story ended there. But Nehemiah reminded them, "The joy of the LORD is your strength" (Nehemiah 8:10). Over and over, God gives gifts of forgiveness, protection, comfort, reward, and joy to those who are sad and in need of answers. Parents of prodigals, too, can find these same gifts, even during setbacks or crises.

Godly Answers

"My thoughts are not your thoughts,
neither are your ways my ways,"
declares the LORD.

ISAIAH 55:8

Each night I lie awake, Lord, praying, pleading with you.
I've done my best to help my child into recovery, but he
is still ensnared. I love my child and wish to see him
live a happy, productive life, but so far, recovery hasn't
come. Everyone seems to have advice, yet none of it
seems to fit our situation. My heart aches for answers—
godly answers.

Lord, you promised Abraham and Sarah a child in their
old age, and the idea seemed so crazy that they laughed.
Yet, in your time, you gave them Isaac. Answers to my
prodigal's troubles sometimes feel impossibly crazy, too,
Lord. When I'm impatient, guard me from forgetting
that miracles and healing are no trouble at all for you.
Strengthen my trust in your timing and your myste-
rious ways, Lord. Let my love grow so that no matter
what, you are my answer.

Yes, No, Not Now

I can see your pain and poverty—constant pain,
dire poverty—but I also see your wealth.

Lord, every day I pray and pray and pray. I pray for my prodigal's healing. I pray for my own healing. I pray every which way, begging for you to answer. Yet I admit that I really only want you to say yes. A "no" or a "not now" answer from you, Lord, feels too hard to bear. I don't want to pray for patience or more courage—it seems like those prayers only turn up the heat, and my circumstances get worse. I'm already at the end of my rope. I'm trying to keep loving my prodigal, even though her behavior takes a jackhammer to my heart. I've tried to be strong, to wait patiently for her to come running home, but I'm growing weaker by the hour. How long must I wait before my prayers are answered with a "yes"?

Father, the longer my prodigal stays on the wrong path, the more I understand prayers with "groanings too deep for words."[3] Instead of being disappointed by a "no" or "not now" answer to prayer, let me see it as an opportunity to draw closer to you. Change my approach from always trying to get something from you to thankfulness for your constant, loving concern for me and my prodigal. As I present my wounded heart to you in prayer, help me enter the peace that passes all understanding. Whether your answer to my prodigal prayer is "yes," "no," or "not now," let me appreciate the wealth I find in you. Lord, thank you for making me spiritually rich in the face of the impoverished grief that a prodigal can bring to the parents who love her.

Refiner's Fire

He knows the way that I take;
when he has tested me, I will come forth as gold.

Job 23:10

I know you want my prodigal made whole as much as I do, and I know you, as a loving God, don't want either of us to suffer. Yet when I think back over my younger years, I see that I learned the most from my many mistakes. Those mistakes were costly and painful—a lot like the lessons my prodigal and I are learning now. When my child's behavior is inconsiderate or dangerous, I can't deny the valuable lesson she's learning from the consequences. If she's irresponsible or immoral, the real world will quickly slap on penalties. And if I speak or act in retaliation, relationships with those I love—my prodigal, my family, even you—will probably suffer too.

Who am I, then, Lord, to question your timing? If I would cut short the tougher life lessons, just to stay pain free, my character and my prodigal's character could stop growing. Just as a smith refines metal to temper and strengthen it, so you sometimes lead your children through fire to strengthen and refine us. Lord, most of us would not willingly jump into your refining fire. When your answer is to plunge my prodigal and I into the flames for our good, help me not resist. Instead, show me and my prodigal ways not just to endure, but to prosper and flourish in spite of the pain.

Joy School

You will give me back my life and give
me wonderful joy in your presence.

Acts 2:28 tlb

When I pray and the situation with my prodigal stays the same, it feels as if you are far away, Lord. How can I be joyful if you're not even interested? At times like these, the many promises of joy sting like alcohol in an open wound. But should my mood depend on how you answer my prayers? Not according to biblical characters who suffered and yet were overflowing with great joy. From Abraham to David to Peter to Paul, your servants found ways to be joyful in the midst of great trials and sufferings. Maybe they were stronger than I am—but maybe they weren't so different from me either.

Father, send me to joy school! In spite of the heartaches that arise when nothing seems to change, help me remember that you work all things together for good. Even when he landed in big trouble, David sang for joy; Paul was tortured and imprisoned and still rejoiced in you. The pain of my prodigal is real and deep and many times takes my breath away. Yet let me grab your joy in strength and weakness, in crisis and peace, at dawn and dusk. When my prodigal starts for home, my joy and gratitude will shine like a supernova. But even when your answer is "wait," remind me that I can always delight in you.

15

Mercy

As parents with strong moral values, we can find ourselves wedged between our wayward prodigal and standing up for what's right. We get caught between staying in a loving relationship with a straying child or holding fast to ideas about right and wrong. If we choose our child, we'll be seen as accepting immoral behavior. If we embrace the right idea, we feel forced to reject our precious child. It's an either-or situation often called "tough love." But what if we could stand for what's right, yet still accept our prodigal?

Somewhere along the way, we adopted the idea that people must earn mercy. When we say our prodigal must deserve mercy, we get stuck in the retributive justice of reward and punishment. Yet God tells us he loves us again and again. He sent his only Son, Jesus, to die for our sins. God's love for everyone—*every* one of us—goes far beyond deserving. Nobody deserves the mercy God freely gives. Mercy takes on a new meaning when we reject retributive love and embrace restorative love.

Gentle Mercy

"This is a hard decision," David replied, "but it is better to fall into the hand of the Lord (for his mercy is great) than into the hands of men."

2 Samuel 24:14 tlb

Lord, you know I was raised by a strict father who passed down what I saw as harsh punishments for my every infraction. That's why I resolved never to berate my own child for spilled milk. But I still ended up seeing you as a stern Father who didn't like anybody very much—and at times I'm as harsh with my prodigals as my earthly father. When my sons lie or neglect responsibilities, my responses are sarcastic and, well, mean. I am so quick to judge—just like good old Dad. The apple doesn't always fall far from the tree, and my critical spirit isn't helping either my prodigals or me find a new way to live.

Lord, thank you that you've led me to see you as a more loving and merciful God. Help me change my critical and judgmental ways so that my prodigals might believe I really do want to help them, not simply enable and then condemn them. As I grow closer to you, God, help me adopt a more merciful attitude toward my prodigals. For your mercy is so much more than pity, Lord. Teach me to adopt a merciful attitude that wants to help my prodigals find healing, instead of an attitude of judgment that writes off anyone who doesn't measure up. Show me how to gently help my prodigals back onto the right path.

A Person, Not a Problem

Blessed are the merciful,
for they will be shown mercy.

Matthew 5:7

They say that when I point a finger at someone, there are three fingers pointing back at me. It's easy to list all the ways my prodigal falls short. All I need to do is display my bullet-riddled heart, my wounded emotions, my dashed dreams. My expectations for this child never included the prodigal problems facing us now. In my private thoughts, I secretly feel disappointment and shame over her. I'm secretly jealous of parents whose kids are successes. I'm angry that parents tend to categorize kids as "good" or "bad." All these raw emotions tend to erupt whenever my prodigal's behavior takes a turn for the worse.

Lord, help me remember that my prodigal never thought she'd be this way either. Her aspirations were as lofty as my own. Forgive my hidden stewing—even if I've never expressed it aloud. When I entertain these thoughts of embarrassment and shame, I deny my child the human dignity you have given to each person. Give me the grace to remember that my prodigal is more than the last bad choice she made. You have shown me great mercy, so teach me to show my prodigal mercy by seeing her as a person, not a problem. A person whom you love.

Flash Point

Have mercy on me, my God, have mercy on me,
for in you I take refuge.
I will take refuge in the shadow of your wings
until the disaster has passed.

Psalm 57:1

When a crisis arises with my prodigal, I go into fight-or-flight mode. My usual levelheadedness disappears and emotions surge. If the situation reaches a flash point, I might find myself holding the phone, wondering if I should call 911. Lord, I don't want my prodigal to get tangled up with the law. He needs help, not a criminal record. Yet if he becomes violent with me or others, I'm forced to bring in outside help. As I hunker down to stay safe until help arrives, my thoughts swing wildly between compassion for my prodigal and my own survival instincts. The whole awful time, my adrenaline pumps and my prayers are reduced to *Help! Help!*

Lord, I hate these kinds of crises, but I'm thankful that you hear my frantic prayers for help. When the danger is past, I want to fall on my knees and praise you for keeping us all safe. Although it's painful, calling in outside help—whether it be the police or doctors or counselors—turns out to be the smartest thing I could do. Give me wisdom, strength, and courage, Father, to make the next right step when chaos breaks out. Have mercy on us all when flash points hit our lives.

Take It Easy

This is what the LORD Almighty said: "Administer true justice; show mercy and compassion to one another."

ZECHARIAH 7:9

When it comes to my prodigal, Lord, I tend to show more mercy to her than to myself. True, it's sometimes more enabling than real mercy, but I'm usually much harder on myself than I am on my grown child. I often mistake protecting and covering up my prodigal's blunders for mercy, but then I beat myself up for not acting more wisely. *Why did I say that? Why didn't I do this?* She deflects attention away from herself by accusing me, and I fall for it. She says, "Mom, you don't do this or say that," and she claims that's why she acts the way she does. My 20/20 hindsight slaps me around for my incompetence and throws in a jab about my neglected duties for good measure. As my self-denigrations go on, I wind up feeling lower than a snail's belly on a slime trail. Then I vow to be better, try harder, do more.

Putting myself down isn't a great way to react to my prodigal, Lord. I need your wisdom to see the truth. Let me take responsibility when I stumble, but help me see through my prodigal's attempts to make everything my fault. The more I criticize myself and my prodigal, the harder it is to show mercy and not rush to judgment. Let your mercy toward me be my guide, Lord, and help me learn to show mercy to myself as much as to my prodigal. Judgment says the case is closed, but mercy says there is still hope.

Comfort

We parents of prodigals can feel overwhelmed a lot of the time. We aren't sure about much. We know we can't change our grown child, but we feel compelled to try. We feel isolated and alone, but we're ashamed to say too much about our situation. We long for our prodigal to come home—but we'd be lost if something bad happened to our child. And during a crisis, pain and hurt and anger and fear swirl together in a dreadful stew of emotion.

That's when the great physician can make all the difference. Jesus wraps his arms around all the hurting places, question marks, regrets, and shame. Our Lord holds us safely while we scream or rage or cry. He is able not only to comfort us, but to be with our prodigal too. Jesus has plenty of love and all the time in the universe. Sometimes the best remedy is made of the courage to hope again, the trust that God is able, and the faith that he will never, ever leave us. Jesus' comfort gets us up in the morning and lies down beside us at night. And his love is big enough to cover parents and prodigals alike.

Deep as the Sea

What can I say for you? With what can I compare you,
Daughter Jerusalem? To what can I liken you,
that I may comfort you, Virgin Daughter Zion?
Your wound is as deep as the sea. Who can heal you?

LAMENTATIONS 2:13

With a prodigal in the family, we parents try everything. If one program doesn't jolt him back onto the right path, we try another. When that fails, someone tells us about a different approach, and we steer that way. With every new strategy, Lord, hope soars and then plummets. We try not to get our hopes up, but we can't help praying that this will be the one. This idea will somehow awaken our prodigal, and he'll forsake all he's been away doing and dash for home. But when the latest suggestion for help doesn't pan out, the downs get deeper. Over time, they carve a painful wound into our hearts—one that can feel as deep as the sea.

Lord, I need your comfort today. More than ever, my prodigal and I need your healing touch. I've grasped at every kind of help I've been offered, hoping that my prodigal would find healing. But he's as far away as ever. As much as I wish for my prodigal's return, when I view the situation through your wisdom, I remember that I can only change myself. Change is hard, but I'll try for you, for my prodigal, for myself. Wrap me in a blanket of comfort and let me rest in your arms, Lord. As I learn how to better relate to my prodigal, spread the comfort of your love over us both—love that is deeper than any sea.

The God Fix

I, even I, am he who comforts you.

ISAIAH 51:12

When my prodigal acts out, I become desperate for comfort. Sometimes I find it during worship in church or by confiding in a trusted friend. I've looked for comfort in songs, in books—even in potato chips or ice cream. Yet wherever I seek comfort in this world from the pain that having a prodigal can bring, the relief is always temporary. I'm not surprised that my heartache returns a few minutes after I polish off that pint of Ben and Jerry's— I'm doing my best, after all. But it's amazing how much like an addict my quest for comfort can be. An addict abuses drugs or alcohol for fleeting relief from the pain, but soon hurts again. I've craved comfort in all the wrong places too.

Time and time again, Father, you hold out your arms to me. Why, then, do I look anywhere else for the comfort that only you can give? Give me a hunger for you, Lord. When my prodigal causes me pain, let me be satisfied only by your comfort. When I'm desperate for relief, hold me back from junk food, numbing media, and other distractions. I pray I'll come to you first, that I might demonstrate to my prodigal where help and hope may be found. When dealing with my prodigal is just too much, let me rest in the shadow of your wings. As I nestle under the soft down of your protection, gather me into your comfort, your wisdom, your love.

A Mother's Love

As a mother comforts her child,
so will I comfort you;
and you will be comforted over Jerusalem.

ISAIAH 66:13

When our prodigal was small, he'd often yell, "Mommy! Daddy!" It didn't matter whether he had an owie, or if something had scared him, or if he was hungry or tired, or if he just had to share. Mommy and Daddy formed the rock upon which his whole world was built. As our prodigal grew more independent, he didn't need us to kiss away boo-boos anymore or listen as he poured out his heart. From adolescence on, he began to look elsewhere for comfort and validation. The rock of Mom and Dad stayed ashore, while our prodigal drifted far out to sea. We waved at him, begging him to come home, but he didn't seem to need or want us in his life. Now he has sailed so far from us that we're the ones who need comfort.

Lord, our prodigal's behavior hurts worse than any skinned knee, yet we often act as if we can't run to you for comfort. Teach us to put aside our parent roles when we come to you in pain. Remind us that we don't have to be strong when we seek the relief that only you can give. Let us feel free to run to you, the God who loves us, crying, "Daddy! Abba! Father!" And as we find comfort in you, renew our hopes so that we will again offer comfort to our prodigal when we spot his sail on the horizon.

Down—but Not Out

*What a wonderful God we have—he is the Father
of our Lord Jesus Christ, the source of every
mercy, and the one who so wonderfully comforts
and strengthens us in our hardships and trials.*

2 Corinthians 1:3-4 tlb

Every day I try to be strong, but then my prodigal says or does something that grieves me, and my heart shatters all over again. People remark that I'm so strong in dealing with my child, but they don't know the reality. I get knocked down, then struggle to my feet, only to get punched again. In my corner between rounds, you comfort me, but I wonder if anything will ever change. It's getting too hard to get back up again—I need help. Others wonder at how well I cope, but you, Lord, know the truth—I'm not coping well at all.

When people say, "I don't know how you do it," let me first acknowledge your goodness, Father. Let me proclaim that when I'm down for the count, my wonderful God's comfort and mercy sustain me. As I deal daily with my prodigal, there's very little that's wonderful— yet you fill me with the strength I need for another round. Each time I'm on the ropes again, breathe new hope into my battered heart. With your comfort, I can both cope and hope.

17

Miracles

We dream of biblical miracles—the kind Jesus performed—for our wayward children. And while miracles do still happen, most aren't the instant, *wow* kind. Instead, a lot of modern miracles unfold slowly, with setbacks and relapses, one step forward and two steps back. Addicts recover, broken families reunite, restitution is repaid—these are miracles too.

What's more, we're often so impatient for a magical, instant healing that we miss the small, everyday miracles happening all around us. A tree leafing out in early spring, a child's laughter, sweet memories of our prodigal in better times—all these can inspire wonder if we let them. And how often do we stop and marvel at the depth of caring and compassion we hold for our prodigals? Whether they turn around in showstopping fashion, or we're asked to keep the candle burning for what feels like far too long, our bonds with our children survive. Maybe the best miracle of all is love.

Sufficient Grace

I will remember the deeds of the LORD;
yes, I will remember your miracles of long ago.

God, you can do *anything*—you created everything, after all. But when it comes to healing my prodigal, matters feel complicated. Sure, Lord, you could zap my kid and presto! She'd be changed. But you also slipped free will into human nature. The story goes that you didn't desire a bunch of robot yes-men, so you gave us choice. Choice which, sadly, my prodigal has used to forge a path into dangerous territory. She stands at the edge of a high waterfall. Another step and she'll plunge into the churning water below. I keep trying to warn her, persuade her to turn back, but she's determined to go over the falls in a barrel. Without a miracle, I fear she'll be gone forever.

Lord, when I read of the great healings in the Bible, it proves to me that you can perform miracles at any time or place you choose. I confess I'm disappointed when my prodigal's situation doesn't seem to rate an instant healing. Teach me your ways, Lord, that I might trust you to keep loving my prodigal. Enlarge my concept of what a miracle can be so that I can keep loving my prodigal even if she refuses to step away from danger. And when I pray for miracles, Father, help me remember the apostle Paul's thorn in the side, and how you said to him, "My grace is sufficient for you."[4]

116   PRAYERS *for* PARENTS *of* PRODIGALS

Signs and Wonders

God always has shown us that these messages are true by
signs and wonders and various miracles and by giving
certain special abilities from the Holy Spirit to those who
believe; yes, God has assigned such gifts to each of us.

HEBREWS 2:4 TLB

When I think of a miracle, I think of supernatural events, like blind people regaining sight or a sea parting its waters. But what exactly is a miracle, anyway? In the twenty-first century, cataracts are routinely surgically removed, and engineers dam rivers for hydroelectric power. What might have seemed miraculous only decades ago now is commonplace. I don't expect my prodigal to dip in a pool and come out healed, but to me, it would be miraculous if he woke up one day and desired to come home to the life he once loved. Although it's not easy to steer away from prayers that seek to change my prodigal, I can pray that I will change.

Lord, I pray I might let go of my overwhelming desire to speed up changes in my prodigal. Help me redirect that miracle spotlight so it shines most brightly on me. Show me where I need to change, even if it's uncomfortable, and let me trust that your Holy Spirit will help me do it gently and in love. Signs and wonders may be different now than in the past, but so much is still the same. Like parents of old, I long for my prodigal to abandon all poor choices and head for home. But Father, I'll need lots of help—changing *my* old habits or attitudes from selfishness and judgment to compassion and love will be a real miracle.

Who's in Charge?

You are the God who performs miracles.

PSALM 77:14

Prodigals with addiction or mental health issues are often urged to go to treatment or take medication to help them become stable community members. We who love these prodigals attend meetings and seek counseling and other tools to help us cope with these issues. But if we agree to give these things a try, what has been shown to cause the most lasting change? Even in nonreligious settings, faith demonstrates staying power that seems to rise above other approaches. As I hold on to you, the one God in three persons, my faith keeps me hoping, loving, and helping in ways nothing else can.

Father, when I'm ready to give up on my prodigal, let me reaffirm my trust in you. No matter how good the counsel or how effective the treatment, human solutions pale in comparison to your loving compassion. Although you could destroy us for our mistakes, you choose to show us mercy. I will take advantage of all the human wisdom available, but your continual kindness toward both my prodigal and me is worth more than anything we humans could devise. Help me remember that you long to show us mercy—a kind of miracle that keeps my hopes alive. I'm so grateful that a loving God is in charge of my life.

A Million Little Miracles

See, I am doing a new thing!
Now it springs up; do you not perceive it?
I am making a way in the wilderness
and streams in the wasteland.

ISAIAH 43:19

The more I focus on that big, splashy miracle I want for my prodigal, the less I'm likely to notice the small, quiet miracles that happen all the time. Some days, it's a miracle that I don't go nuts and jump out a window. Other days, my prodigal shows a glimmer of the person I know and love—a smile, a kind gesture, an "I love you." Those things, too, are miracles—miracles I know that you, Father, send to keep me from despair. The smallest glimpses of you when I'm about to give up on my prodigal are miracles that feed me like nothing else can.

When unseen angels protect me on the highway, or my prodigal miraculously survives a brush with danger or death, you are right there in the middle of it, Lord. Help me remember that you also feed me tiny bits of sunshine every day—in a stranger's smile, a warm breeze, those peeks of goodness into my prodigal I sometimes get. If my prodigal does or says something positive, let me be grateful—but help me not pile all my hopes into that one basket. Thank you, Lord, for your beautiful and complex creation, a balm for my bruised and battered heart. Let me relish the million little miracles, for there is where I will find you, and that's where I want to be.

18

Trust

We all tend to separate God from this earthly life. We think of our lives as "down here" and God as "up there." But is it true? If our creator made everything, then he is part of everything. So when we put our trust in God, it doesn't need to mean we reject all earthly solutions and remedies for our prodigal. Yes, some men hold evil intent, and it can be difficult to discern if God is in the midst of a particular help. How can we know for sure?

Start by using God's love and the Scriptures as the ultimate tests. If you believe God in all matters, you know he is trustworthy. With humans, it's wise to always search for what they do and not just what they say. Look for verification in prayer and in the world. Yes, evil is real. But with prayer and some fact finding, we parents of prodigals can trust God and get guidance. His love can come from the counselor's lips, the doctor's prescription pad, or even a stranger's helping hand.

Learning to Trust God

The LORD is good,
a refuge in times of trouble.
He cares for those who trust in him.

NAHUM 1:7

If I trust, *really* trust your plan for me and my child, I'll see that my dashed hopes often stem from what *I* wanted to happen, *when* I wanted it to happen. I want to fix the situation because it's not easy to see my child behaving in ways that hurt everyone. It's painful to go through trials that these actions generate, and it's heartbreaking to watch the fallout. If my child suffers, I suffer too.

Lord, give me faith to trust you. Help me surrender everything, even my tendency to hope for outcomes according to my human timing. Strengthen my faith in the truth that you want the best for my prodigal and me. Help me trust in your timing. Then my hope—growing, vital, alive—may even spread to those around me, lifting us out of worry and disappointment and sailing us to the shores of love. As I learn to truly trust in you, may others remark, "Your hope gives me hope."

Carry Me Through

*You saw how the LORD your God carried
you, as a father carries his son, all the way
you went until you reached this place.*

DEUTERONOMY 1:31

Sometimes it's hard to see how, in the desert, the Israelites kept forgetting how much you wanted to help them. When my prodigal stumbles, I want to rush in and make everything okay again. And as I ache for my child, I glimpse the pain you must have felt whenever the Israelites strayed. So often I, too, let worry or busyness interfere with reading my Bible and spending time with you. Being human, I'm prone to forget that you have been carrying me all along.

Lord, when I'm down for the count, point me back to the Bible. Then help me remember to look up, to see that your love triumphs no matter how bad my circumstances seem. When my heart has practically turned to mush from all the disasters, there you are, helping me up with a nail-scarred hand, reminding me that you are no stranger to suffering. I'm so grateful that you carry me—and my precious child too. Lord, when I forget how much you care, strengthen me with the Scriptures.

Whom Do You Love?

I trust in your unfailing love;
my heart rejoices in your salvation.

PSALM 13:5

When my prodigal speaks or acts in a way that makes me cringe, it hurts—in a special way only parents can know. The worst of all is when he shouts, "I hate you!" It's hard to keep quiet when your heart shatters like delicate crystal. When I recently reached out to others for comfort, complaining about my prodigal's latest insult, my friends told me how much you love me. It was reassuring, yet one friend said the best thing: "Don't forget that God loves your prodigal just as much as you." She reminded me that just as I will never stop loving my prodigal, you never stop loving him either.

Lord, when I feel as if I cannot bear another moment of my precious child's absence—whether physical or otherwise—remind me that I can trust you never to stop loving either of us. This empty place where my prodigal should be keeps getting wider and deeper with each passing day, yet I know you hold each of us in the palm of your hand. Give me the grace to trust that your ways are perfect. We may be far from perfect ourselves, but thank you for sending a good word in my time of need. Whenever I think I'm not going to make it, help me trust in your love for me, my prodigal, and the world.

God Catches Me

Do not let your hearts be troubled. You
believe in God; believe also in me.

John 14:1

That team-building trust exercise where you fall backward, believing others will catch you, reminds me of the way I worry about trusting my prodigal. She often lies or skirts the truth about things she doesn't want me to know, but now and then she is honest. Then the next time, I'm never sure if I can fall and know she'll catch me, or if I'll smack the pavement. Some call this "walking on eggshells"—I never know what will happen to set her off—but it's really about trust. If I can't trust her to relate to me honestly, how can I trust her in anything? If I doubt my prodigal will deal authentically with me, I start to form a sad opinion of who she is.

God, I don't want to think of my child in a jaded or cynical way. When the light shines on our wrong choices, we all naturally try to protect ourselves. Those who are self-protecting—including my prodigal—go on the defensive because they know their path is leading away from you. Help me view their struggle not from a high perch on the mountain of goodness, but as a fellow human who sometimes gets defensive too. Give me insight to see my prodigal as the hurt, scared, and lonely person she must be. Help me see past *my* pain to her pain. I need your wisdom to show compassion *and* set boundaries that I can stick by. Let me put my trust in you and you alone—so I can fall backward, knowing you will always catch me in your loving arms.

19

Grace

We often don't understand why we have a prodigal. It's tempting for us to ask God, "Why me?" We can list a thousand ways why God shouldn't have saddled us with such a burden. It's very human to want God to remove a trial from us, and everybody complains now and then. But we parents of prodigals don't want to miss out on God's grace either.

Joni Eareckson Tada has been a quadriplegic since her teens. If anyone deserves to complain to God, she does. Joni's not perfect, yet she doesn't spend a lot of time asking God, "Why me?" Instead, she says, "Grace always, always meets us at our point of pain!"[5] When we see our struggles this way, we realize that in our pain with our prodigal, we get extra-large helpings of grace—grace to endure, grace to pray, grace to love. And if we look into the midst of grace, we'll see the face of Jesus loving us back.

In Living Color

*The law was given through Moses; grace
and truth came through Jesus Christ.*

JOHN 1:17

Sometimes I admit that I see my prodigal in black and white. Until the day my prodigal stops walking the wrong path and starts toward home, she's either doing right or not doing right. I often find myself thinking, *That's not how we raised you! You know what's right—there's no excuse for what you are doing!* In my mind, the dangers of her life choices require fast action. I rush at warp speed, past grace and right into legal territory. Then, if my prodigal gets in trouble with the police, the law seems more important than ever. In our society, there's no gray area—you're either guilty or innocent. I hate seeing life in black and white, especially when it comes to labeling my prodigal child, whom I love so much.

Lord, I know it's not right to label people. Reducing anyone—including my own prodigal—to an either-or label only gives fear a chance to grow in me. My head knows we're all complicated and in need of grace, but fear tricks me into thinking that anyone who knows the right way and doesn't follow it deserves punishment without mercy. Lord, strengthen my resolve to be a grace giver more than a law enforcer. Grow my love so that I might cast out the fear that wants to divide and separate, condemn and punish. Show me how to better love my prodigal and all people until I can extend grace that sees in living color.

A Furious Grace

Let us come boldly to the very throne of God
and stay there to receive his mercy and to
find grace to help us in our times of need.

Hebrews 4:16 TLB

The last time we spoke, my prodigal and I got into another shouting match. We both yelled hurtful words, and neither of us heard the other's position. We stayed as deadlocked as politicians from opposite ends of the spectrum, until, finally, my prodigal stomped out. I stood there, shaking and red faced and still sure I was 100 percent right. If I'd had the nerve to go to your throne room right then, I'd have admitted that neither my prodigal nor I was loving and that at least one of us was wrong. At that time, I was so angry that I didn't want grace or mercy—only what I thought was justice. And justice had to include a punishment that would make my prodigal concede that I was right.

Lord, my righteous indignation didn't solve anything—and may have made the situation worse. Even if I could sit on my prodigal until he yells uncle, I'd still be trying to force him to change. Help me remember that being right is good, but that grace and mercy are the tools you choose to deal with your people. Help me invest as much energy into calmly loving my prodigal as I have in being angry and right. Untie my ideas about justice from my emotions and instead fix my gaze on the mercy and humble grace you freely give to everyone who asks.

In times of need—like family arguments—help me swap my righteous anger for the peace that passes all understanding. Lord, let me lay aside judgments and take up grace—even when I know I'm right.

A "Peace" of Grace

Grace to you and peace from God our
Father and the Lord Jesus Christ.

PHILEMON 3 RSV

You know, I haven't had a good night's sleep in ages.
I think, pray, and worry about my prodigal's behavior,
sometimes into the wee hours. Some nights I replay a
recent argument in my mind and try to figure out why
our emotions got so heated. Other times tears drip onto
my pillow after my prodigal's latest dose of silent treatment. Either way, I lie in the dark, pleading with you
for this long ordeal to be over. Even when I'm reading
scriptures, inside I'm spinning so fast, I'm afraid I'll go
careening out into space. How do I show grace when
my prodigal is so sinful and wrong? But you often link
grace with peace. Suddenly, the picture is clear: When
I focus on my prodigal's wrongs, peace escapes me, and
grace never crosses my mind.

Lord, I crave the peace that passes all understanding.
Cleanse my tendency to think only of my prodigal's mistakes and the consequences of those sins. Concentrating
only on punishment agitates my emotions and hardens
my heart. I want to see my prodigal as you do, Father,
with many good qualities alongside the wrongs I see so
clearly. Help me encourage my prodigal instead of crit-
icizing, treating her with respect rather than judgment,

giving her a smile instead of a scowl. Let peace quiet the turmoil within me and let me offer that peace to my child. With your help, I'll cradle the grace you give me each day and then pass it on to my prodigal.

What Grace Is Made Of

I will praise the LORD no matter what happens. I
will constantly speak of his glories and grace.

PSALM 34:1 TLB

What if my prodigal gets put in jail? What if he dies?
When I pray for healing for my child, I'm hoping you
will save him from a terrible fate. As one of his parents, I want to spare him from suffering. As he's strayed
down this troubled path, a dangerous maze, I've had to
watch him run a gauntlet of poor choices and decisions.
I'm always hoping he'll turn around before the worst
happens, like losing his job, his home, his family, his
freedom, or, heaven forbid, his life. I know I can't force
him to change. But I'd do anything to keep him from
suffering more loss. I'd do anything to keep him alive.
And to me, it seems like your grace should protect my
prodigal the same way that I would.

God, all through history your people have lost homes,
loved ones, and freedom. While it's more than scary to
think of losing my precious prodigal child, my pleas
to spare him suffering may not be the kind of grace
you have in mind for him. Strengthen my trust in your
goodness, Lord. If, like the Israelites, my child loses
his home, grant me grace to see that he may need that
strong of a wake-up call. If, like the apostle Paul, my
child is thrown into prison, remind me that you are

there, right beside him. Give me the wisdom I need to allow my prodigal the experiences—positive or negative—that are part of your plan for his life. Reassure me that your grace is like a parent's love—deep and true and strong.

20

Endurance

An old joke goes, "How does a mother change a lightbulb?" Answer: She doesn't—she says, "I'll just sit here in the dark." We parents know we might wait a long time before our prodigal heads home. We're in it for the long haul. Yet having a prodigal doesn't mean we should forfeit our own lives. How much time do we spend worrying, doing errands for, or obsessing about our kids? Too much, perhaps?

We're loving, compassionate people, and we know how to delay—really delay—gratification. But we don't have to sit in the dark. While we'll always be concerned over our prodigal's welfare, we aren't bad parents if we take some time to find joy in our own lives. Jesus came to give us life abundantly. Open the windows of your prodigal-centered existence and let his light flood in.

How Long?

How long, LORD, must I call for help,
but you do not listen?

HABAKKUK 1:2

Why don't you heal my prodigal, Lord? I keep trying to figure it out. Is there some prayer I didn't pray? Something I forgot to do? I rack my brain for the key that will unlock a miracle, but so far, it hasn't arrived. My soul groans in anguish as I watch my prodigal waste his life on harmful pleasures. I don't get why you haven't healed him. I find myself thinking, "How long, God?"

Lord, I fall at your feet. As my prodigal's waywardness continues, help me seek your face. Help me remember that my prodigal's troubles seem awful and never-ending, but you, too, know what it's like to be in agony for what must have felt like forever. You willingly endured the cross for me and my prodigal, so I know you really *do* understand. Help me lean on you in bad times and in good, to keep hoping for that miracle despite appearances. Help me change my "How long?" attitude into one of joyfully abiding in you.

War of Words

I endure scorn for your sake,
and shame covers my face.

PSALM 69:7

If I try to persuade my prodigal to leave behind her troubling ways, we usually end up arguing. When my grown child feels threatened, she goes on the attack—and often, so do I. The twin blades of sarcasm and disrespect come out, and we trade blows of insult, each of us poking at the other's soft spots. My prodigal's put-downs and name-calling are but a smoke screen for the real issue. My snappy comebacks try to shield me from hurt and establish parental authority. Our battle tactics don't accomplish much. We both slink away under a stench of scorn and shame.

God, I don't want to be stuck in a war of endurance with my prodigal. When we play this cruel version of "last man standing," we lose valuable time—time when we could be communicating instead of talking (or shouting) at each other. Give me grace to slow down and listen to my prodigal—really listen. Give me peace to remain calm if she goes on the defensive. Show my prodigal that, as I lay down my weapons of scorn and shame, it's safe for her to do so too. Help us treat each other with respect, to defeat scorn and shame at the root.

One Step at a Time

*Since we are surrounded by such a great cloud of
witnesses, let us throw off everything that hinders and
the sin that so easily entangles. And let us run with
perseverance the race marked out for us, fixing our
eyes on Jesus, the pioneer and perfecter of faith.*

HEBREWS 12:1-2

You know I've never been good at running, Lord. With
my asthma, I passed out while jogging on the school
track back in seventh grade. I never wanted to be a parent of a prodigal, either, and I don't feel any better at it
than running. As the months and years of this prodigal trial stretch on, I often complain that I can't make
it another minute. "It's so not fair," I cry. I hate being
left out whenever I hear of a prodigal coming home
while my child is still out there somewhere. But I shud-
der when I learn of someone's prodigal going to prison
or overdosing. A parent of a prodigal suffers too much
pain, worry, guilt, and sadness. Nobody in their right
mind would sign up for this kind of race—even for a
free T-shirt.

Lord, you marked this race out for me, and so often I
want to drop out or take a shortcut. Yet I think of Jesus,
and that bolsters my determination. And I remember
how, even when I passed out in seventh grade, I came to,
got on my feet, and made it across the finish line. The
longer my prodigal stays away, the more overwhelming

the racecourse seems. I can't do it—at least not until I look up and see Jesus running alongside me, loving me every step of the way. And if I faint on the track, I know he will carry me a while. Father, help me keep my gaze on Jesus Christ, the author and finisher of my faith.

Strength for the Journey Home

As for me, I watch in hope for the LORD,
I wait for God my Savior; my God will hear me.

MICAH 7:7

My heart knows I can't endure until my prodigal turns around, and my head still thinks it's all up to me. My every waking thought seems to cycle through feelings of exhaustion and despair, pep talks to keep myself going, and then more feelings of deflation, like I'm a flat tire. I might pat myself on the back for surviving the latest crisis or for not enabling my prodigal. But when things go wrong again (and they always do), I'm apt to pick out my mistakes and obsess over ways I might do better next time. I cry out to you for help, then I go right back to flying solo—thinking I must get through this prodigal mess in my own strength.

Lord, I don't understand why I forget that true endurance comes not from my own efforts, but from you. When the going gets tough, let me cry out for your protection. When I think I can't hang on, help me grab your outstretched hand. When my prodigal's behavior blasts new wounds into my deepest places, remind me that you are no stranger to suffering. Let me write on my heart the truth of your enduring love. And please, Lord, shower your loving-kindness on my prodigal, for she'll need strength for the journey home.

21

Courage

Halftime in a football game means the players go into the locker room to rest for a few minutes. Yet the biggest reason for halftime is the coach's pep talk. Pep talks renew the team's courage. If they're losing, the coach convinces them they can win. If they're ahead, the coach cautions against growing complacent.

Parents of prodigals experience these same ups and downs with their courage. To cope with a prodigal every day for months, years, and even decades takes focus, stamina, and courage—which can wane when we fear we're losing our child or become boastful or prideful when we think we're winning. When your courage is running low, run to God's locker room and open the Bible for a pep talk. "Take courage...for I am with you," our heavenly coach reminds us (Haggai 2:4 NASB). With fresh courage, we can trot back onto the field, ready to kick off another round.

Courage, Not Fear

*No one had the courage to speak out for him in
public for fear of reprisals from the Jewish leaders.*

JOHN 7:13 TLB

They say it's useless to reason with someone who is under
the influence. But when my prodigal sobers up or is acting "normal," I feel tongue tied. Instead of confronting my
prodigal about his unacceptable behavior, I tend to want
to hang on to this lull like it's a much-needed vacation. In
the middle of a crisis, I think of all sorts of things I want my
prodigal to hear—boundaries I am setting, plans for sanity,
demands that he do something to help himself. The problem is, he can't and won't hear anything while he's under
the sway of his current direction. I don't speak up for fear
of losing what little relationship we have left. My courage slips through my fingers like water until the next crisis.

Boy, I could sure use some courage today. Jesus' admirers
were scared to back him up for fear they'd be targeted too.
I often feel this way about my child. If I am unwilling
to speak truth to my prodigal, it's because I fear he will
either start a big to-do or else cut me out of his life completely. Lord, I pray you will grant me courage so that I
can face my prodigal in truth. Give me the right words
and the right place and time to "tell it like it is." Grow my
trust in you so that I can give thanks for those moments
when my prodigal sees more clearly. And when I falter
under the weight of fear, pick me up, Lord, and send me
out again, armed with your courage and love.

Courage to Accept

God has not given us a spirit of timidity,
but of power and love and discipline.

2 Timothy 1:7 nasb

I'd do anything for my child—fight off a man-eating shark, brave rogue waves, keep her head above water until she's back ashore. The one area where I'm not so brave is in acceptance. I'm strong in praying for my prodigal's deliverance, Lord. It's easy for me to stand up and crusade for what's right and against what's wrong. But as I flex my courageous muscles, I find my prodigal becoming tangled in the net of my righteous indignation. Since my prodigal paddled off the safe swimmers' beach and dove into shark-infested waters, I've been shocked, repulsed, in despair, and close to hopeless. The farther she's traveled away from me, the more I feel like a swimmer caught in a riptide. The harder I try to get her to safety, the faster my prodigal steams out to sea. When she says my efforts to save her from evil have convinced her that I think she's bad, my heart sinks to the depths.

Father, you know my intentions. In my zeal for taking a stand against wrongdoing, I never expected my prodigal to see my courage as rejection. Give me the wisdom and self-discipline to accept my prodigal *before* she turns away from those dangerous waters. Let me imitate Jesus, who doesn't require us to change so that he can love us but loves us so that we *can* change. Let my love for my child—that fierce I'd-do-anything-for-you love—be on full display to my prodigal. Even as I continue to pray and hope for her deliverance, give me courage to accept her the way she is right now.

Broken Arrow

*I refresh the humble and give new courage to
those with repentant hearts.*

Isaiah 57:15 TLB

I'm a straight arrow—I don't like risk taking, and I play
by the rules. In some ways I'm good at "being good." My
prodigal, though, flirts with danger every day. I don't get
why he goes out on the spindliest limb he can find—so
far, treatment hasn't helped, nor has legal punishment
or even social shunning. If I had to give up the diet soda
I love or else go to jail, I'd pour all my two-liters down
the drain, pronto. But both offers of help and threats of
punishment seem to bounce off my prodigal. Things
that cause me to rush to the changing room only appear
to annoy him.

Lord, on the outside my prodigal seems to resist change.
But, thankfully, you look at the heart. When I'm full of
my upstanding ways, am I being courageous or simply
prideful? In running from attempts to correct him, is my
child being stubborn or fearful? Stop me from thinking
of my child as an extension of myself. He is the unique
individual you made him to be! Let me not forget that
what's easy for me might be nearly impossible for my
prodigal. You knew him before he was formed in the
womb, God. Help me take a step back so that I might
humbly see with new courage and new eyes. Give me a
repentant heart that sees my prodigal not as broken, but
as a precious arrow, one fashioned by the creator of all.

Healing Courage

Be strong and courageous, and do the
work. Don't be afraid or discouraged, for
the LORD God, my God, is with you.

1 CHRONICLES 28:20 NLT

Much of the time I'm focused on my prodigal and the changes I think she needs to make. I read, go to counselors and group therapy, and pray, always concentrating on my prodigal's behavior or condition. But there was that one day a treatment counselor looked at me and asked, "Do you know how sick you are?" I felt as if I'd been punched in the gut. Me? Sick? *No, no,* I thought, *this counselor has it all wrong.* Except that she was right. Over years of dealing with my prodigal's issues, I'd grown a giant cancer, a tumor that kept me from seeing my own sickness as part of a dysfunctional family. I learned to keep secrets, keep quiet, keep on enabling. I'd thought I was sailing toward my prodigal's problems. All the while I was bounding across a sea of fear, riding the waves on a ship named *Shame.*

Lord, I need courage. Courage to continue dealing with my prodigal, but also courage to face my weaknesses. If I'm sick, I'll pray for your healing touch. If I'm scared, I'll let you lead the way into battle. If I'm discouraged, I'll read your promises. Don't let me forget that if you are with me, you are with my prodigal too. When you walk with me, Lord God, it's possible to face my fears, to do the hard work that changing myself entails. As I draw from you the strength and courage to change, I pray my prodigal will see that with you, impossible things can and do happen. Thank you, Jesus—the best doctor, who heals us when we don't even realize we're sick.

22

Self-Care

When my prodigal was a baby, I sacrificed everything for his welfare. I didn't sleep, eat, or shower much in those newborn days. As he grew, I still found myself putting his needs before my own. I cut his meat, wiped his nose, and controlled his life. Yet, somehow, I missed the memo that he's all grown up now and can take care of himself. Even as he wanders far away, my parental instincts want to make everything all better for this now-grown child.

What message do I send my prodigal whenever I rush in to fix or rescue? That he's incapable of taking care of himself? I want my grown child to be an independent and successful adult, so I'll need to cut the cord. He's come to rely on my over-parenting, so it may not be easy. But with God's help, I'll let him go. I'll hold my breath as he fledges, but I know God will catch him if he falls.

I Parent So Hard

You have searched me, LORD,
and you know me.
You know when I sit and when I rise;
you perceive my thoughts from afar.

PSALM 139:1-2

They say, "Nobody likes a martyr." I grew up in a household where the unspoken rule was that *Mom eats last*. If she wanted a cookie from a near-empty box, she never ate the last one. As a parent of a prodigal, I often martyr myself this same way. I sacrifice my time, money, and resources to give to a grown child who often doesn't say thanks. Or when we have little to no contact, I spend my waking hours worrying over my prodigal's whereabouts and well-being. And while I often believe I am "nurturing" my child, in truth I am sucking the life out of my own well-being. I know my prodigal isn't a baby anymore, yet I keep attending to every need as if he were helpless. In neglecting myself, I court resentment, burnout, and bitterness.

Lord, you know my thoughts—thoughts that always urge me to rush to help my child. But when I don't take care of myself because I've spent everything on my prodigal, you also see the damage to my body, mind, and spirit. Reach into my heart, Lord. Give me just the right amount of self-regard—let me know it's okay to take the last cookie now and then. Let me serve others gladly, but only from a healthy perspective. Show me a better way than too much self-sacrificing to cope with my prodigal. Transform me, Father, from a false martyr to someone who cares enough to take care of myself too. Rather than chasing eventual resentment and burnout, I want to show myself the same love I pour out for you, my family, and my prodigal.

Never Obsolete

*Do not conform to the pattern of this world, but be
transformed by the renewing of your mind. Then
you will be able to test and approve what God's
will is—his good, pleasing and perfect will.*

ROMANS 12:2

I rush about, trying to please my prodigal and everyone else. I feel awful if my efforts aren't appreciated,
but secretly I believe that if I just do a little more, a little better, then my child (and everyone else) will love
me. Yet no matter how much I do for my grown child,
it's never enough. I didn't raise him to be demanding,
sullen, and critical, but that's how he acts with me. His
once generous and positive outlook has been replaced
by that of a grumpy grinch, always finding something
to complain about, something more he needs. And he
always needs it right now. I keep thinking I can satisfy him by running faster, giving more, being more,
like that superwoman in Proverbs 31. But deep down,
I know the truth: People pleasers can never satisfy anyone—including themselves.

Lord, the truth about trying to please my prodigal—
that it's impossible—stops me short. It's not about being
a super-parent, as I've told myself. I'm so afraid of not
being needed that I try to make sure it never happens.
Help me see that to you, I will never be obsolete. Halt
my busyness and allow your love and compassion to
pour into the well of my heart. Renew my mind to

think of my prodigal as capable, smart, and perfectly able to take care of his own life. As I make more time for me, show me what work you would have me do. I love you, Lord. Help me learn to let my prodigal go so I might take care of myself too.

You Do You

The Lord will work out his plans for my life—
for your loving-kindness, Lord, continues forever.
Don't abandon me—for you made me.

Psalm 138:8 TLB

I'm finding that sometimes the kindest thing is to do nothing. I often spend so much on my grown child that there's nothing left over. Afraid I'll be abandoned or rejected, I lavish my resources on items my prodigal should provide for herself—if only she weren't caught up in the trap of waywardness. But if I'm honest, allowing my grown child to face consequences is just too painful to think about. So I bail her out while my teeth fail, my clothes tatter, my priorities turn upside down—all while convincing myself that I don't really need much of anything.

Lord, reset my priorities. Help me see how failure can build character, how consequences can teach my prodigal. I don't really want to rob her of such rich life experiences. And I certainly don't want to pity my prodigal. Help me stay in my own circle, Lord. Let me see more clearly your plans for *my* life. Guide me to attend to my own needs with the same energy that I've shown to my grown child. I raised her as best I could, Lord. Loosen my grip on her life and keep me from intervening to the detriment of my health and well-being. Father, let me "do me" and allow my prodigal to own her own life as I step back in love.

Love's Bumper Sticker

It is God who works in you to will and to
act in order to fulfill his good purpose.

<small>PHILIPPIANS 2:13</small>

I know you are with me, God—the Bible says so. Yet as I deal with my prodigal daily, it often feels as if I'm in this alone. The weight of the world is so heavy on my shoulders—the worry, the guilt, the shame that having a prodigal brings. I cringe when I see those bumper stickers bragging about honor students and the glowing Christmas letters from parents of successful, awesome children. They remind me that, as a parent, I haven't raised my child in "the way he should go."[6] I cry out to you, Lord, that I tried really, really hard. And then I hang my head. I'm ashamed. I don't like myself much. How could you like me?

When I'm self-loathing, let me draw close to you, the God of all love. The God of compassion and loving-kindness, of mercy and comfort. Take away the thoughts that I don't measure up. Assure me of your love. Remind me that my prodigal is now grown—making decisions, walking a path of his own choosing. If I erred in raising him, instead of self-denigration, let me forgive myself. You are love, which neither condemns nor casts me away. As I walk with you, Father, help me keep my head up—and let me rejoice with the parents of those kids with bumper-sticker accomplishments instead of resenting them. Guide me to find and give thanks for all the goodness life has to offer as I listen for your voice in everything I do.

23

Letting Go

Letting go sounds a lot easier than it is. We parents give our prodigals to God over and over, only to grab them back. Yet you might reach a point where you're either too tired or too weak to be the boss of the situation a moment longer. You haven't stopped loving. You've only stopped trying to control another person's life.

But when that person is your child, it's so much harder. You might move across the country from your abusive parents, your alcoholic husband, or your addicted uncle or cousin. Detaching from your offspring takes much more resolve. They will always be your child, no matter what. You'll always love them. To keep these things yet let go of prodigal problems sounds impossible. And it would be, if God weren't there to step in where you've failed. Attend a meeting, find a prayer partner, see a counselor. Keep on giving your prodigals to God, as many times as it takes.

The Path to Letting Go

*I am letting them go their blind and stubborn
way, living according to their own desires.*

PSALM 81:12 TLB

One of the hardest things about having a prodigal is separating the sin from the sinner. Loving my grown child, yet hating the path she's chosen, brings out my nurturing instincts. I often try to overprotect my prodigal like a mother grizzly, totally ignoring the fact that my child is now an adult. Other times I'm in so much pain that I turn my back, claiming I can't watch my prodigal harm herself any longer. Either way I deny my prodigal the opportunity to change. I can't seem to let go without micromanaging or judging, when accepting my prodigal where she's at would surely make it easier to let go and trust you, God.

I love walking with you. I long for my grown child to walk with you, too, so much so that I forget how my own path to you wasn't always straight or smooth. My prodigal's current direction saddens and frightens me, and, so far, nothing I've said or done has changed her mind. I love her as only a parent can, but I need your help to let her go. Help me remember that my prodigal needs my love and acceptance more than my advice or protection. Keep me focused on love—for you and my precious prodigal. Let me love my grown child the way you love me, Lord. No matter what, you will never abandon me. Even as my prodigal walks through the valley of the shadow, you will be with her. In letting her go with true love and acceptance, I'll be there for her too.

Bless and Let Go

The Man said, "Let me go, for it is dawn." But Jacob panted, "I will not let you go until you bless me."

GENESIS 32:26 TLB

As the weeks, months, and years pass, letting go of my prodigal seems impossible. If I let go, this child I love will surely fall into the abyss and be gone forever. I've prayed and begged you for answers for so long—too long. Yet my prodigal grows nearer to the edge of doom, with no end in sight. Instead of dawn's arrival, life with a prodigal seems like endless night. In the darkness I run ahead of my child like a human flashlight, hoping against hope that he'll see the light and turn toward home. But so far he only keeps running—away from me, away from safety. All I can think to do is grab a fistful of his coat and hold on tight. Why, God, are you so silent? If I let my prodigal go, I'm afraid I'll also lose the last shred of hope.

Father, you know my actions arise from fear—fear of the unknown, fear that my grown child will be swallowed up by darkness, fear that you somehow can't hear my pleas. Yet I know that in the silence, you are there. Show me that, even in the black of night, your light will always shine for prodigals and those who love them. Give me courage to see that you, God, love my prodigal much more than I ever could. Help me embrace your promise that if I release my tight hold on my grown child, I'll receive a blessing. I'll be able to stop trying to change my prodigal with my puny flashlight, and your holy light can shine more brightly into his life.

Seek Understanding

God gave Solomon wisdom and very great
insight, and a breadth of understanding as
measureless as the sand on the seashore.

1 Kings 4:29

In the past, I haven't understood why my prodigal couldn't simply let go of his destructive path. I thought my grown child was simply rebellious, making poor choices or neglecting his upbringing. If he knew better but was only *choosing* this lifestyle, then punishment surely would make him stop. But what if he doesn't willingly choose? What if his brain is different from most? The more scientists learn about the human brain, the more I understand how addiction, mental illness, and a host of other conditions can change a life. What appears as a simple choice to me is really a brain condition— one that cannot choose avoidance so easily. In our fallen state, we're all in need of God's forgiveness, but the more we know about how the mind and body works, a rush to judgment may fade and God's mercy may increase.

Lord, thank you for creating my precious child, from his fingers and toes to his brain. I would never judge my child if he had a common condition like diabetes or a heart problem. Maybe my prodigal's brain processes life differently—even if I punish him, he doesn't stop. Help me see the world the way my prodigal sees. Grant me wisdom and understanding as to why he can't seem to walk away from the dangerous path he's on. Comfort us both when we suffer and pour out your Spirit as we seek the truth. Be that lamp unto our feet as we make choices. Help us both let go of mistaken ideas and guide us into love for each other.

A Prayer for Letting Go

*Brothers and sisters, I do not consider myself yet to
have taken hold of it. But one thing I do: Forgetting
what is behind and straining toward what is ahead, I
press on toward the goal to win the prize for which
God has called me heavenward in Christ Jesus.*

PHILIPPIANS 3:13-14

Lord, when it comes to letting go of my prodigal, so
often I've messed up. I've held on tightly when I should
have nudged her out of the nest to fly into her adult
life. I've ignored so many opportunities to let her learn
and grow through her problems and trials. Instead, I've
taken over, rescued, and enabled. Every time my grown
child has cried out, I've rushed to her side as if she were
helpless. I can't seem to keep boundaries, use tough
love, or detach from my prodigal's problems. I want to
be a good parent, but I seem to make these same mistakes again and again.

God, maybe what I need to let go of is perfection, and
maybe what I should embrace is prayer. I've messed up
with my prodigal—and I confess that all to you. But
that was yesterday. Today's a new chance for a fresh start,
one that doesn't lean on my own strength, but upon you,
Lord. To lean on you, I'll meet you in prayer. Open my
eyes, Lord, that I might find my way to my prayer closet
before I race to enable or rescue. Give me a desire to talk

everything over with you, Father, before I do anything else. Help me strain toward what is ahead—prayer that will set free both prodigal and parent—as I release, like chaff into the wind, all of yesterday's mistakes.

24

Peace

Peace. We parents of prodigals don't seem to get much. With a prodigal, there's always something new—a new crisis, new development, new argument—pinching our toes as well as our relationship. We tell ourselves we can handle the stress the prodigal scatters across our path, but our shoes wear thin, and our feet become cut and bruised by our grown child's sticks and stones. Even our human attempts at peace, like a cardboard sole, are no match for the long journey we must make. Soon blisters appear, and we believe that peace is just a day without drama.

Real peace is so much more than the absence of conflict. Jesus promises to leave us peace that passes all understanding (see Philippians 4:6-7)—a deep knowing that God is in control, that we don't need to feel afraid. As we put on the armor of God, we can slip on shoes of "readiness that comes from the gospel of peace" (Ephesians 6:15). Shod with the peace of the Lord, we parents of prodigals can better run the race set before us. Who knows? Our prodigal may notice our stylish footwear and want in on this peace that's like no other.

Pride and Peace

Tell [Phinehas] I am making my covenant of peace with him.

NUMBERS 25:12

For so long, I couldn't even talk about my prodigal without getting upset. I threw around poison words, blamed and argued—all in righteous indignation. I punished my prodigal with shame, guilted him into a corner, and browbeat my own grown child with my fervent beliefs. Being right and rubbing it into my prodigal's open wounds felt good—for a little while. But soon I began to feel like the Pharisee who prayed aloud that he was better than others.[7] Instead of walking in a calm, spring-breeze kind of peace, loveless gale-force winds kept me off balance. Time and again, my pride in being right has made a bad situation unbearable. Worse, all the finger pointing has stolen my peace.

Lord, I want to be an instrument of your peace. My prodigal's situation is bad, but I don't have to make it worse. Seal my lips when I reach for unkind words. Replace indignation with compassion and help me understand that all the rightness in the world is no substitute for love. Show me ways to pour kindness into my prodigal's wounds and help me snuff out the candle of pride that urges me to think more highly of myself than I should. You made a covenant of peace with Phinehas, Lord. Fill me with your holiness and love, that I might extend mercy to my child and be at peace with my prodigal, myself, and you.

Peace for My Prodigal

*Nevertheless, I will bring health and healing
to it; I will heal my people and will let them
enjoy abundant peace and security.*

JEREMIAH 33:6

While I desire peace in this chaotic life with a prodigal, I know my grown child needs peace even more than I do. The cravings of an addict, the rejection and isolation of a frowned-upon lifestyle, or the loss of faith—this dark forest surely inflicts deeper suffering on him than I can comprehend. Add to that the puzzling ways he reacts—nothing seems to lessen his commitment to the desolate path he walks. Loss of family, health, jobs; being threatened with jail; possible overdosing or drug violence…all of that scares the socks off me. But my prodigal walks farther into the thick brush, despite all the dangerous possibilities lying in wait. For my child or any prodigal, peace must be elusive.

Lord, even as I ask for your peace, my prodigal needs you even more than I do. Help my precious but lost child find his way to you, God. Instead of judgment, let him see your mercy. Show him that you are waiting quietly for him. The dangerous woods he travels hide hungry beasts that want to consume him, but if he looks up, he'll see a loving God in the small clearing. Bring my prodigal to that place, Lord. Quiet his fearful heart long enough to hear your voice. Help me provide a trail of bread crumbs that leads straight to your meadow of peace. And Lord, let my prodigal finally understand that you long for him—not to punish him, but to give him life. Perhaps then he can lay down his troubles and embrace the peace you freely offer to all.

Peace that Pampers

Do not be anxious about anything, but in every
situation, by prayer and petition, with thanksgiving,
present your requests to God. And the peace of God,
which transcends all understanding, will guard
your hearts and your minds in Christ Jesus.

Philippians 4:6-7

My constant anxiety over my prodigal keeps peace away—I worry about the other shoe dropping at any moment. My broken heart's jagged little pieces poke holes through my prayers, and I'm hurting so badly that I forget to be thankful. In this crazy life with a prodigal, it seems that every day I do things for my grown child—things she could do for herself. But I often refuse to do nice or restoring acts for myself—like I don't deserve to feel good unless my life is peaceful. I give so much to everyone else that there's nothing left for me. When I daydream about peace, Lord, I think of taking a deep breath and letting it out—relaxing at a lovely day spa or the beach, hiking a beautiful trail, leisurely enjoying a meal. These pleasures seem so far out of reach, along with any sort of lasting peace.

Lord, sometimes it's so hard to love myself. Underneath all my excuses, I blame myself for my prodigal's behavior. Peace seems to slip through my fingers, and my anxiety goes through the roof, but that's not how you want me to live. Keep me praying, asking you to heal both my prodigal and me. Keep me thankful too—a grateful heart has a harder time worrying. When I'm stingy with myself, lead me to the place of gratitude for everything in my life. If I hesitate to pamper myself now and then, remind me of your love for me. Remind me that if I don't bankrupt my resources on others, including my prodigal, I'll have something left in order to show myself the same loving concern I show to others. Thank you, dear Lord, for your peace in my life.

The Peace Rose

*Peace I leave with you; my peace I give you. I
do not give to you as the world gives. Do not let
your hearts be troubled and do not be afraid.*

JOHN 14:27

I recall that June day, walking around my garden, holding my breath, waiting for something awful to happen with my prodigal. Even though my garden grows a delicate pink-and-yellow Peace rose, I still dreaded the worst. Bad situations had arisen with my prodigal in the past. It felt like something more could happen any minute. My heart was troubled—I couldn't wait another moment for you to answer my prayers for my prodigal's healing.

I've tried and tried to change my prodigal—leaving self-help books in conspicuous places, making unasked-for suggestions, giving not-so-subtle hints of what I long to see. My efforts to "help" my grown child have only wilted and, even now, my prodigal's rejections gouge me like thorns. I can't find peace, no matter how hard I look.

Lord, I want your peace—it's different from and far better than the peace of the world. Your peace is more like knowing the thorn may draw blood, but you will be covering my wound with love. Your beautiful creation assures me that you may not deliver my prodigal or me this instant, but your peace gives me strength and

courage. Peace helps me stand strong and keep on praying, keep on loving. Thank you, Jesus, for the wonderful
gift of peace. Like the flowers in my garden, your peace's
fragrance and vibrant beauty help me calm down, let
out my breath, and take time to smell the roses.

25

Love

When it comes to my prodigals, love is confusing, infuriating, and the best thing ever. I love my sons so deeply, yet a swirl of competing emotions leaves me out of breath. I love my grown children, and yet at times I wish I could hang them up by their toenails too. I'd fight to protect my prodigals, but when they act in ways I don't approve of or believe in, I'm tempted to throw them out on the street. Love and hate, hate and love. My feelings seem caught in a whirlpool with no way out.

But maybe love isn't just an action that I do or don't do. Maybe love is what and who I *am*. Love is inside me, and it is beyond me. I can say, "I love." But when I *am* love, I'm connected to God in a way that feels abundant, giving me a well that will never run dry. This kind of love doesn't come and go, depending on circumstances. No, love is patient and kind, keeping no record of wrongs (1 Corinthians 13:4-5). The love of God frees parents and prodigals alike to love one another despite our failures, our addictions, our differences. Love is hope's flame, the hope that my prodigals and your prodigals and everyone's prodigals will find their way back home. Soon.

God Loves Prodigals

"My son," the father said, "you are always with
me, and everything I have is yours."

LUKE 15:31

So much of the time, my prodigal is so unlovable. It's hard not to be angry or to cut her off after she's broken my trust again and again. My first instinct is to punish, to cause as much pain as she's caused all our loved ones. Even if she isn't physically violent, words and actions hurt too. Well-meaning friends and family want to protect me, so they say her behavior proves that she deserves punishment.

Thank you, Lord, for your everlasting love. No matter what, you haven't cut me off or turned your back on me. Even though I deserve nothing but punishment, when I turn back to you, you open your arms wide—just like the biblical father of the prodigal son. Help me remember that you accept me just as I am and that, even if my prodigal is far away, squandering her life, you don't reject her either. To you, my child is much more than the last bad thing she did. Help me hear your still, small voice, Lord. Teach me to love as you love, in wisdom and compassion.

Where Do I End?

*Be devoted to one another in love. Honor
one another above yourselves.*

ROMANS 12:10

God, you know how deeply I love my prodigal. But sometimes it's hard for me to tell where my child ends and where I begin. I spend so much of my day thinking about my prodigal, coming up with ideas on how to help, and, I admit, beating myself up when these helpful ideas don't work. Simply put, when he suffers, I suffer. I'm supposed to form boundaries and stand firm. People counsel me not to fall for my prodigal's manipulations. And yet again and again you urge me to care. To serve. To love. I need help to find the balance between my devotion to my prodigal and staying healthy myself.

Father, I get so confused about how to love others—especially my prodigal. Help me accept that some of what I think is love for my prodigal is really rooted in pride—pride in thinking that I can live my child's life better than he can. I surrender that pride, Lord. Show me *your* way of honoring others above myself in this me-centered world. Help me understand when healthy love for my prodigal becomes obsession, where devotion to this child has put blinders on my eyes. Let me walk humbly with Jesus as I help myself to a grace that can love without enabling or rescuing. Teach me how to love without losing myself.

The Lens of Love

This is my command: Love each other.

JOHN 15:17

Why does my child keep on doing the very things that hurt all of us—especially when he's been given many chances to stop? If I don't enforce conditions and consequences on our relationship, how will my prodigal ever be motivated to change? How do I love someone who continues in a destructive lifestyle or who isn't trying to change? Hating the sin but loving the sinner is so hard—especially when it's your own child.

Lord, maybe I'm thinking too much about the hate and sin part, and not enough about loving the sinner. Let me focus on you so that it's easier to locate my heart, and let me keep my heart soft with loving compassion. Help me view my prodigal and everyone I meet through the lens of love—love that knows that, but by your grace, I'd suffer the same sin sickness. Give me a hunger to love others as I would be loved.

Love You Forever

Now these three remain: faith, hope and
love. But the greatest of these is love.

1 Corinthians 13:13

So often I dispense love according to who I believe deserves it. If my prodigal is inching my way or doing something I approve of, love for him gushes out in torrents. But when he isn't following my idea of righteousness, I tend to withhold that love. Maybe I give my prodigal the silent treatment. Maybe I gouge him with my sarcastic remarks. Or maybe I simply stand on a metaphorical corner and loudly thank you that I'm not as bad as he is. I don't mean to be so fickle—it's the hurt that activates my defenses. Broken promises, broken trust, broken heart—these three reminders of past slights bring out the worst in me. I've been burned, so I'm cautious about giving away my love.

Father, time and again, you take my brokenness and mend it with your amazing love. You never withdraw your love. Forgive my human tendency to think love is only good for good people. As I learn more about my prodigal's path, help me let go of myths, traditions, or lore that base love on rewards and punishments. I don't understand or approve of where my child is at, but if I love the way Jesus teaches us, I cannot withdraw my love until my prodigal straightens up. I've been protecting my heart from more pain, but that same protection keeps me from loving freely. If I'm following Jesus, I'll keep my heart open, even if my child never comes back to where I want him to be. Because of you, Lord, I'll love my prodigal today, tomorrow, and forever.

Acknowledgments

On days when you're sure all hope is lost, a book of prayers might not seem like much of an answer. But in writing these short supplications, I found more comfort than I ever thought possible. Thanks to my editor Terry Glaspey, who understands. Thanks to my agent, Nick Harrison, for believing in my story. Thanks to my steadfast friends of the Advanced Writer's Group: Tamsin, Jodi, Mo, and Jenny. Thanks to long-time buddies Heather Harpham Kopp and Melody Carlson, and to my writing partner and fellow burned-popcorn lover, Kay Marshall Strom. Special thanks to my family, for all they put up with from me. And thanks be to our Lord Jesus Christ for unfailing love that carries me through. I love you all.

Notes

1. Job 38:4.

2. Matthew 5:38.

3. Romans 8:26 ESV.

4. 2 Corinthians 12:9.

5. Joni Eareckson Tada with Larry Libby, *A Spectacle of Glory* (Grand Rapids, MI: Zondervan, 2016), 57. Find daily devotions on Joni's website at https://www.joni-andfriends.org/category/daily-devotional.

6. Proverbs 22:6 NASB.

7. See Luke 18:9-14.

About the Author

Linda S. Clare is the author and coauthor of several books, including *The Fence My Father Built* and *A Sky Without Stars*. Her articles have appeared in *Chicken Soup, Cup of Comfort,* and *Guideposts* anthologies. Linda teaches writing at Lane Community College and is a regular speaker at writer's conferences.

Library of Congress Cataloging-in-Publication Data

Names: Clare, Linda, author.
Title: Prayers for parents of prodigals / Linda Clare.
Description: Eugene : Harvest House Publishers, 2020.
Identifiers: LCCN 2019027322 (print) | LCCN 2019027323 (ebook) | ISBN
   9780736979016 (trade paperback) | ISBN 9780736979023 (ebook)
Subjects: LCSH: Parents--Religious life. | Prayers. | Intercessory
   prayer--Christianity.. | Problem children--Prayers and devotions.
Classification: LCC BV4529 .C5175 2020 (print) | LCC BV4529 (ebook) | DDC
   242/.645--dc23
LC record available at https://lccn.loc.gov/2019027322
LC ebook record available at https://lccn.loc.gov/2019027323

To learn more about Harvest House books and
to read sample chapters, visit our website:

www.harvesthousepublishers.com

HARVEST HOUSE PUBLISHERS
EUGENE, OREGON